The History and Virtues of Cyder

Roger French was born in Coventry and educated at King Henry VIII School. He studied zoology at St Catherine's College, Oxford and took a D.Phil. in the history of science, working on medicine in the eighteenth century. He was a lecturer in the history of science at the Universities of Leicester and Aberdeen and lecturer and Director of the Wellcome Unit for the History of Medicine at the University of Cambridge.

This book is the result of a combination of academic research and practical experience: Roger bought a cider-mill cottage in the 1960s where he made, and drank, a great deal of cider, recovering centuries-old techniques and preserving old varieties of cider fruit. He died in 2002.

D1144134

The History and Virtues of Cyder

R K FRENCH

ROBERT HALE LIMITED
London

© R.K. French 1982
First published in Great Britain 1982
Paperback edition 2010

ISBN 978-0-7090-9122-6

Robert Hale Limited
Clerkenwell House
Clerkenwell Green
London EC1R 0HT

www.halebooks.com

The right of R.K. French to be identified as author of
this work has been asserted by him in accordance
with the Copyright, Designs and Patents Act 1988

A catalogue record for this book is available from the British Library

10 9 8 7 6 5 4 3 2 1

Printed in Great Britain by the MPG Books Group, Bodmin and King's Lynn

Foreword

'Deep in the countryside something is stirring. Along the Marches of the Welsh border, down in Devon and Somerset people are pulling from old barns and forgotten corners pieces of strange machinery, large and old. They are tightening the hoops on dry and dusty hogsheads. What is happening? They have rediscovered cyder.'

In the years that have passed since my father wrote these words and this book, there has been a renaissance in all things cyder. His plea for the production of quality cyder has to some extent been answered. Such cyder producers as Tom Oliver, Jean Nowell of Lyne Down, James Marsden of Gregg's Pit, Kevin Minchew of Gloucestershire and Julian Temperley in Somerset, to name but a few, have, in recent years, led the way in producing wonderful cyders and perries. They have been an inspiration to many. Exciting publications, such as James Crowden's *Ciderland*, reflect the growing enthusiasm and skilful methods of the modern cyderist.

What has caused this renaissance? Growing concerns about the provenance and production of what we eat and drink has led to a rebirth of real ale and cyder. Cyder's market share has recently seen a vast increase supported by the campaign for real ale. Such organisations as The Three Counties Cider and Perry Association, The Big Apple and Common Ground continue to promote and support real cyder and its makers as well as the preservation and replanting of traditional orchards. This book inspired many of them, and has a firm place in cyder's renaissance.

Edmund French
Cyder Maker

Contents

Part Three

Illustrations

The author thanks the following for permission to reproduce pictures: the Hereford Reference Library, the Wellcome Trustees, Hereford Times Ltd, and the Clarendon Press for the illustrations from *A History of Technology*

Part One

The title-page of Worlidge's *Vinetum Britannicum* of 1676, an
important treatise

Introductory

Cyder is no longer made. This book shows why not, and why it should be: what cyder is, how to make it and how to enjoy it. It is a plea for Real Cyder. We are all familiar with pasteurized, diluted, bland and carbon-dioxide-injected cider, but cyder is a living wine of some subtlety, matured in cask and bottle in the manner of champagne. The reputation of cider is now past the low point of an ebb it has suffered for a century or more, and it is timely to reintroduce English readers to an old English drink. Moreover, with increasing demand for apple juice and new orcharding techniques, it is now again economically possible for the prospective cyderist, like his seventeenth-century forebear, to select and purchase a plot of land, to plant and care for his trees; and room can be found in any garden for the new, cheap and prolific bush trees for the amateur to make his own cyder.

In subsequent sections we shall see that at its seventeenth-century height, cyder was a *wine*, not a long drink. At its best it was often preferred to good French white wine, and in England there was much discussion on how cyder should best be made. It was the landowner, with a choice of orchards and fruit, who experimented and kept the best for himself and his family. The production of cyder soon became a cottage industry, and the modest householder with a small orchard could still enjoy an excellent wine from his own land. But in the eighteenth century the industry was gradually taken over by the cider merchants who bought the fresh juice, not the final product, and practised all manner of sophistications upon it to obtain as much of the final drink from as little of the juice as possible. By now, too, the farmer and landowner had taken to giving his farmhands cider as part of their wages, and like the merchant he found it a satis-factory arrangement to keep the best of the cyder for himself and

3

The orchard gives way to pasture: as the small cider producers were squeezed out of business, their cottages and orchards were bought by farmers who raised Hereford cattle. Frequently cottage and mill were abandoned, or else the stone mills were pulled from the cottages and left lying in the fields in pieces

dilute the rest to make it go further; or he would make cider from what was left of his fruit after the first extraction of the juice by the addition of water. During the nineteenth century cyder entered its long decline: from the farms, cottages and merchants, its production passed into the hands of larger and larger firms, and the old stone mills and wooden presses became idle; the farmer and landowner no longer drank his own cyder but preferred imported wines, which for political, economic and social reasons were readily available. The tradition of making real cyder died when gentlemen stopped drinking it. Cider is still made by isolated individuals in various villages in the West Country today, but invariably the product is at least half water: it is the survival of what the farmhands and household servants drank, but in no sense is it real cyder.

The origins of cyder

To understand more clearly what cyder was, why it vanished, and why and how to make it, we must first look at its early history.

We cannot tell of course when cyder was first made, any more than we can describe the first production of wine. Apples have a geographical northern limit roughly equivalent to that of grapes, and it is merely an historical accident that wine is no longer produced in large quantities in the cider counties of south-west England (although the situation is being rapidly corrected). Wine and cyder are predominantly drinks of the South therefore, while the colder more northern countries have historically depended on beer and ale, the products of grain. Within historical times cyder emerged as pre-eminently a Celtic drink, associated with them from their profoundest antiquity, and no doubt brought by them from their southern origins. The Celtic "Britons" came to Britain long before the Romans are said[1] to have introduced the apple tree, and the poetry of their descendants, the Welsh, contains ecstatic descriptions of the apple tree, and no one interested in folklore need be reminded of druids, sacred groves and mistletoe, which depends on the apple tree for its existence.

All that we know about cyder at this early period was that it was a drink made from apples. We cannot tell how it was made, and whether water was added. To distinguish between cyder and cider, we need to know these things, or at least the strength of the product. All that would be a guide to us on this score are some drinking stories surviving from classical antiquity, and these make it seem probable that we cannot rely on the accuracy of the fabled quantities consumed by the heroes of old. Only one fact makes it worth while to repeat such stories, and that is that they were known to those who were looking for the ideal cyder and ways of making it at the beginning of the modern period. Worlidge, a central figure in the seventeenth-century English renaissance of cyder, recalled a story from Pliny that exceptionally gifted topers of his day could drink three gallons of wine at a draught. Pliny knew of cyder,[2] but gives us no information that would be useful in comparing its strength in Roman times with that of Roman wine. Cyder was more popular among the Greeks than the Romans and from the Greek world we hear further details of the "three-gallon man": William Harvey, the younger countryman of Worlidge and the discoverer of the circulation of the blood, was in the habit, while lecturing on anatomy to the College of Physicians, of retelling the story of Alexander the Great's drinking competition.[3] Many of the competitors died during the contest or shortly after, but Torquatus Tricongius survived long enough to take the prize, having drunk his twenty-four pints.

Two interesting points emerge from these stories. The first is that we must obviously suspect that the figures have been exaggerated as the stories were repeated. A *congius* was an eighth of an emphora, about six pints, so "Tricongius" was the name of a man who could drink three of them (Cicero's son was known as Bicongius, "Two-gallon Tully"). But the stories also say that the wine was not diluted, and that the competitors consumed it *at a draught*, without drawing breath between gulps. It seems unlikely that we can rely entirely on the quantitative details of ancient accounts of drink and drinking. Secondly, the stories were taken much more literally by people in the sixteenth and seventeenth centuries, including those who were considering the problems of cyder production.[4] Recognizing that the ancient feats of drinking were unlikely to be repeated by modern man, the physicians of the Renaissance sought an explanation in the idea, not uncommon at the time, that modern man was smaller and more feeble, both physically and intellectually, than his Greek and Roman ancestors. Had not the Fall from paradise, combined with man's addiction to vice of every kind, caused his body to degenerate physically? Many anatomists certainly thought so, including Harvey. Their evidence was on the one hand the detailed account of anatomy left by the second-century Greek anatomist Galen and, on the other, the appearance of the dissected human body in the university anatomy theatre. But Galen had in fact not dissected men, but apes. The species of ape involved had a breastbone of seven parts, while the anatomists of the Renaissance could find only five in man. Sylvius, the great Parisian anatomist of the mid-sixteenth century, not unnaturally concluded that this was an example of degeneration. The big, seven-boned chest of ancient man, he said, clearly had a vastly greater capacity and enormous lungs: this was the reason, announced Sylvius confidently, that Torquatus was able to drink twenty-four pints of wine without drawing breath; and why Hercules could run round the stadium carrying an ox over his head, on one breath.[5]

The medieval western world, after the collapse of the ancient civilizations, drew its knowledge of science and technology from two sources; first, a direct inheritance from what the Romans knew of Greek culture, preserved by the Latin-speaking church and, second, from an extended contact with the Arabs, who had overrun Alexandria and were hard by Byzantium. The Arabs, in other words, had direct access to Greek ideas of antiquity and these began to pass to the West with increasing frequency after the twelfth century. Cyder fits into this picture of science and society like other achievements of civilization. It was at first made in the West without any sophistication, from unselected fruit in a haphazard manner. No doubt this was an inheritance from Rome, where cider had been neglected because of the preference for wine. Serious cultivation of the apple and pear did not take place in the West before the fifth century, and before that cider makers were obliged to depend on the customary eating apple, the qualities of which could not have been suitable for cyder, and on wild or crab apples, some of which may well have had a suitably astringent flavour but which also, doubtless, were inclined to acidity, and certainly had a low sugar content. This first cider and perry in the West were *poor* men's drinks; St Guénolé (414–504) of Brittany (famous in a later period for its cyder) chose to chastise himself by living on a diet of water and perry, and other ascetics in the sixth and seventh centuries, braver still, chastised themselves by living on perry alone. Undoubtedly such perry (and cider) was made with a great deal of water, and was not cyder in our sense. It was most likely made in the manner of *dépense*, a drink made by allowing slices of apples, grapes and other fruit to ferment in water; there are regulations of Charlemagne governing the brewing of such drinks. Even as late as the sixteenth century Parisians were making *dépense* by pouring water over lacerated apples and waiting for the exuding

7

juice to ferment.

Cider making of this kind exemplifies the poverty of the domestic western tradition. It is true that some improvements in the technique were made, most likely following the attention given to cultivation of varieties of fruit in the fifth century. By the seventh century Normandy cider was apparently good enough to be offered at a meal alongside wine, for we read that it was given to St Columbanus by Thierry II, King of Burgundy and Orleans. But real improvement had to wait for the introduction of more highly cultivated varieties from the East.[6] Possibly the source was the generous climate of some Arabic lands, Moorish Spain or North Africa. Bad apple crops in a later period in France were supplemented by imports from the Bay of Biscay; we

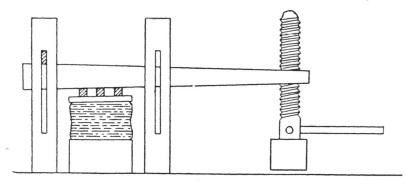

Fruit presses of antiquity. The ancient producer of wine and olive oil resorted to a number of mechanical contrivances to exert pressure on the milled fruit that were very similar to those used by the eighteenth-century cyderist. In the press where a beam acts as a lever, the primitive device of hanging a weight on the end of the beam was replaced by a large wooden screw, as in the presses described by Pliny, which we see *above* and *below*

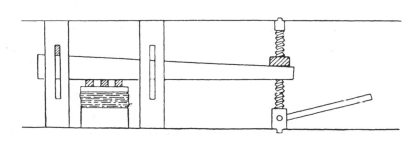

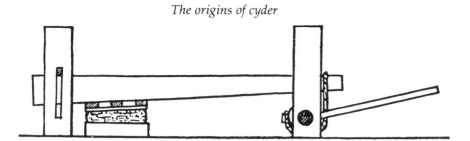

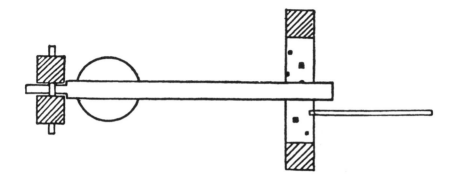

Alternatively, a capstan was used in place of the screw, as in the press described by Cato (*above*), sometimes with the additional advantage of a block and tackle (*below*). In Cato's press the beam was up to 50 feet long; in a block-and-tackle press it was about 30 feet long

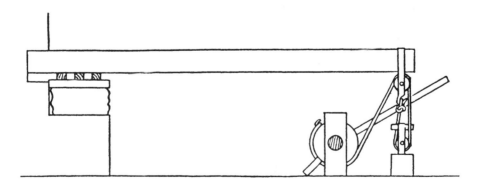

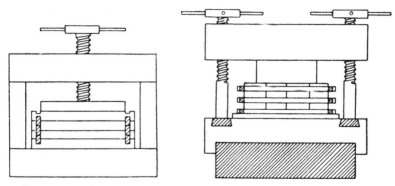

The pressure from screws could be applied directly to the milled fruit. These single- and twin-screw presses, described by Hero (first century A.D.), are similar to the cyder presses of the later West. These illustrations should be compared with those reproduced later in the book from seventeenth- and eighteenth-century sources

cannot claim that cyder, like science, returned to the West through Arabic hands, but it is certainly true, as we shall see later, that the varieties of apple suitable for cyder are very late in ripening, which is suggestive of an origin in a warmer climate. More importantly, the equipment used in milling and pressing cyder fruit can be confidently traced back to that used in dealing with olives. France, of the European countries, developed the art of making cyder during the Middle Ages, taking their cue either from the Arabs in Spain[7] or the olive-growing areas of the Mediterranean. The real development began during the eleventh century, when new communications, including the crusades, were opened up between East and West.

By the twelfth century there is evidence of cultivation of apples in Spain, and the non-European Basques, bordering both Spain and France, had a well-established tradition of cyder making. So despite the traditional association of cyder with the Celts, the evidence seems to suggest that the technology, the cultivation of the fruit and the habit of drinking cyder came into western Christendom from Moorish Spain. From France the habit came to England after the Conquest.

Linguistic considerations also suggest a movement of the cyder habit from East to West. "Cyder" is a word that occurs in almost all the Indo-European languages, a group that stretches from Scandinavia to India, but it seems to have existed for longer in those languages of the warmer regions of the group. The modern English "cider" (spelled "cyder" almost universally until the nineteenth century) was derived, at about the time we are now discussing, from the Middle English *sidre* which itself was derived from an Old French word of the same spelling. The word in Old French probably represents, and is almost certainly cognate with, the late Latin *sicera* (in Greek *sikera*) which was used in the septuagint as a translation of the Hebrew *shēkār*, which indeed seems cognate with it. When Wyclif translated the "strong drink" of the Bible as "cider", it was probably on the basis of the language of the original, and because of the strength of the cider he knew.

To summarize, we have evidence from the earlier Middle Ages in the West of a native cider made with water and the crudest of juice-extraction techniques practised upon wild or unselected fruit, and of an imported method of making cyder made from specially cultivated fruit. Only with the machinery and techniques borrowed from wine and olive-oil production can the juice be satisfactorily extracted from apples, and it is not an unreasonable guess that this apple juice, like that of grapes and olives, was used as it came from the press, without the addition of water.

The later Middle Ages

The development of the cyder habit in England dates from the thirteenth century, when the cultivation of new varieties of apple was well established, having been borrowed from Normandy.[8] Already Devon was a cyder-producing area,[9] but cyder trees were by no means restricted to the West Country, and

11

Giraldus Cambrensis tells us that the monks of Canterbury preferred cyder to Kentish ale.[10] The point of Giraldus's tale is that the Canterbury monks were luxurious in their tastes, and so we must suppose that their cyder was a drink of some sophistication, easily displacing the older, native cider. We naturally also suppose that the monks were drinking their own, or locally produced, cyder: some evidence of the quantities of English cyder made in the twelfth century can be gathered from the Pipe Rolls of Henry II. On the other hand, at an early date cyder was shipped from port to port. This means not only that it had good keeping qualities, but also, because of the economics of shipment, that it was much more likely to have been a drink with the strength of wine: both pointers to it having been real cyder. A third piece of evidence for this is formed by the scattered records of cyder mills and presses, without which cyder cannot be made.

These three kinds of evidence also show that by the thirteenth century there were the beginnings of a cyder industry in England. By 1212, cyder was a source of income for Battle Abbey, perhaps from its estates on the Wye, which ran through land that by the fourteenth century was producing a good deal of cyder. During this time, too, cyder was imported from Normandy; large quantities of Normandy cyder were being shipped to Winchelsea around 1270. Five years later there is a record of a legal entanglement centred on a cyder mill and press in east Sussex. Again, in 1313, at the same place, a tenant farmer of the archbishop's estates had to account for twelve shillings spent on four casks, repairing the press, and the wages of men engaged in making cyder.[11] By 1341, as many as 74 of the 80 parishes in west Sussex were paying tithes of cyder to the church, and 29 also in the form of apples. Such tithes were of considerable value, being 100 shillings at "Easebourne" and £6/13/4 at Wisborough. Rents as well as tithes could be paid in kind, for we hear that at about the same time the tenant of the manor of Runham in Norfolk held it *in capite* by two *mues* of "wine made of permains" paid into the exchequer of Edward 1 (1274–1307) each Michaelmas.[12] ("Permains" were known as such soon after 1200[13]). Likewise the records of the exchequer make reference to land held in Norfolk on a rent, payable in hogsheads, of "wine made of pearmains", which is used in these records as a synonym of "cyder".

Cyder was becoming a commodity: a valuable means of exchange, worth the effort of transportation, strong enough to remain unspoilt in cask from Michaelmas to Michaelmas, stable enough to be shipped abroad, and needing expensive machinery for its production.

All this is evidence of cyder of wine strength. The conclusive evidence relates to the weight of fruit used to produce a given volume of cyder: in 1282 the bailiff of Cowick stated in his account that he had made sixty gallons from just over three quarters of fruit, and early in the next century we read that ten quarters of apples produced a tun (tonel) of cyder as rent. A tun may be reckoned to be the equivalent of two *pipes*, each of which in turn comprised two hogsheads, in all, something over 240 gallons. While some caution must be exercised in interpreting these figures, because volumetric measures vary considerably from place to place, from trade to trade and with time, it is not unreasonable to conclude that a ton of apples produced rather less than 100 gallons of cyder. This agrees very well with modern figures for undiluted apple juice straight from the cyder press. The alcohol content of this after fermentation is high, and we may see the justice of Wyclif's translation.

Seventeenth-century English cyder

The seventeenth century was the heyday of English cyder, and it was often thought of as the wine of England. But in different places and for different reasons, cyder was often "stretched" by the addition of water. When the habit became widespread as a means of paying workmen, the knell of real cyder was sounded; but before that happened the two drinks co-existed, albeit having different purposes.

One of the earliest pieces of evidence we have is from the herbalist Parkinson, who tells us that in the early seventeenth century cyder was often mixed with water for consumption on board ship.[14] It was probably recognized that cyder helps to avoid scurvy, and this is dealt with below: what interests us here is that this mixture of cyder and water was known as "beverage", the forerunner of many different kinds of weak cider, or cyder-and-water; the weakness of "beverage" is indicated by the early application of the term to such drinks as lemonade.[15]

Diluting a finished cyder with water to produce beverage was less frequent than re-working the milled fruit that had already produced a strong cyder. The "small perry" that had been known since the days of Piers Plowman (who called it "piri-whit")[16] was probably made in some such way, and in the early seventeenth century we find explicit rules for making "small cider" from the ground fruit that has already produced strong cyder: Gervase Markham says:

> Now after you have prest all, you shall save that which is within the hair cloth bag, and putting it into several vessels, pour a pretty quantity of Water there-unto, and after it hath stood a day or two, and hath been well stirred together, presse it also over again, for this will make a small Perry or Cider, and must be spent first.[17]

Whether or not water was added to cyder depended to a certain extent on where it was made. In Jersey even the very strongest cyder, carefully made from the first-pressings (see below) had a bucket of water added to every hogshead, in the belief that it improved the fermentation, and there was no cider at all upon the island without some added water.[18] Beale tells us that some kinds of apples make a cool "small Wine" with water added at grinding, but that other fruit, like that of Longhope in Hereford-shire, cannot stand the addition of water without turning sour.[19] Water was commonly added during grinding of apples that were over-ripe in order to prevent too rapid a fermentation: one of Evelyn's correspondents says six gallons was added to every twenty bushels of apples – that is, the resulting cider was about one third water.[20]

The names used for these weaker ciders probably indicate their widespread origins. Whereas "beverage" commonly meant cyder-and-water, it seems in the West Country to have meant the result of a second pressing of watered pummice (ground fruit). Perhaps the term "small cider" is the best to cover all the forms of weak cider: it is a term that was introduced in analogy with "small beer",[21] that is, a beer which was produced from a second working of the malted barley that had already produced a "strong ale". Now, the weakness of small cider and small beer meant that they did not keep so long as real cyder and strong ale, and some means of preserving them had to be found. The beverage which in Devon was weak juice that was finally and with great effort expressed from the pummice was preserved by the addition of spices.[22] Sometimes it was boiled before the addition of spices, and sometimes hops were used to prolong its life. It is an interesting possibility that the same reasons lay behind the growth of both common cider and of bitter beer: true ale contains no hops, and it was only in the sixteenth century that hops were imported and used in beer, perhaps primarily to extend the life of small beer, in the same way that spices and hops were used in small cider. Because of the inferiority of their materials, small beer and small cider were cheap and so popular among the poor. More importantly, as we shall see below, servants and labourers came to be paid partly in small beer and small cider, and demand for these products, coupled with the habit of the upper classes of drinking imported wine, led to the disappearance of unhopped strong ale and real cyder.

The lower orders of society were drinking some form of dilute cider and beer at least as early as the middle of the seventeenth century. Evelyn says it was the habit of the citizens (of London) to drink "*six-shilling* Beer" diluted, and of the "*honest* Countrymen" to drink diluted cyder: he was told by the "labouring People" that they worked much better upon weak cider than best beer.[23] It was sound economic sense to provide small cider for the servants: although it was not formally part of a labourer's wages until the eighteenth century, the living-in servant of the seventeenth century had to be fed and supplied with drink; making cyder for the master of the house and his family left materials that would simply be wasted unless re-used for small cider; small cider did not keep and so in season, could be drunk in quantity; the use of small cider in place of small beer also saved fuel in brewing, and grain for the making of bread, advantages which on a national scale were not lost upon Evelyn and other members of the Royal Society.

The eighteenth-century authors[24] also give us details of weak ciders, normally made by allowing the once-pressed "murc" to stand for up to a week with the added water. The strength of the resulting cider is fairly indicated by the name "washings" sometimes employed. The term "ciderkin" preferred by Worlidge in the previous century now seems to have been supplanted by "beverage".[25] The diminutive ending "-kin", so aptly used in "ciderkin", came to be used also in the eighteenth century in "pirkin", a term meaning "small cider" and apparently coined from the seventeenth-century term "purre", also meaning "small cider". Perhaps, too, "purre" also appears in yet another eighteenth-century name for small cider, "pomepirk". The diminutive of this, "pomepirkin", was in use at least as early as the 1630s to indicate a *watered* cider, not one made from re-pressing the murc. Often enough spare apples and a small quantity of good cyder or its lees would be added to small cider.

Sound evidence of the strength of cider and some other drinks in the first half of the eighteenth century is provided by a physiological writer[26] who, in the fashion of the time, imagined the human body to be simply a collection of tubes, a "hydraulic engine". His interest lay in discovering how far up various small pipes different fluids would rise by "attraction" or capillarity, and he duly noted down his experimental results with a variety of biological fluids and also cider, small beer, common ale, red wine, punch, brandy and spirit of wine. He noted the density of them all, taking, like the modern wine-maker, the density of cold water to be 1000. Alcohol is lighter than water and so the stronger the drink, the further below 1000 is its specific gravity, or "density" in eighteenth-century terms. Thus our writer's double-distilled spirit of wine was measured at 823, very much stronger than the brandy at 932. The standard we are looking for is provided by his figure for red wine, 993: it must have been very dry and very strong. The lightness of the alcohol in the mixture is counterbalanced by the weight of dissolved solids like grape sugar in sweet wines and malt products in beer, and so we cannot tell precisely the strength of a drink without knowing the *original* specific gravity before fermentation. However, it is unlikely that a dry cyder would contain more dissolved solids than a dry red wine, and it would have been very much lighter than the figure of 1011 for this example of eighteenth-century cider; the same figure is given for small beer, which we know to have been made from spent materials, so that its weight came from the small proportion of alcohol and the high proportion of dissolved solids (common ale was 1030, the solids from the richer source materials completely masking the alcohol). We may guess, using the same arguments, that cider was weak and had also gained weight by the addition of sugar or other materials to make it palatable.

Scientific evidence of the strength of the common cider of the Somerset labourer in the second half of the nineteenth century is provided by the analysis made by the German scientist Voelcker: by weight, 4.16 per cent of it was alcohol, that is, about the strength of beer today, and far less than that of wine-strength cyder.[27] This cider was part of the labourer's wages, and he made up for its lack of strength by the volume he drank. In Herefordshire at about the same time the masters gave their labourers about six pints a day, and at harvest-time many labourers would drink as many as twenty or twenty-four pints during the course of a working day.[28] It cannot have been very strong; although we cannot tell from these accounts whether the Somerset or Herefordshire cider was "small cider" or diluted cider made in the modern manner, its weakness prevented it from keeping well, and the Herefordshire labourers preferred cider so sour that it tasted like vinegar to strangers. (In contrast, Voelcker's analysis showed no acetic acid in the Somerset cider.) The labourer's attitude to his cider as part of his wages is preserved in the Herefordshire story of the labourer who asked his master for an extra ration of cider because it was so bad.

It was only in the nineteenth century, when the great apples of the seventeenth century had all but disappeared, that techniques became available for measuring the strength of cyder; but we are fortunate in having two sources where the question of strength, including that of the old varieties, was tackled. The first of these is the Herefordian Thomas Knight, who made use

17

of the new chemistry of the early nineteenth century, and the second is *The Herefordshire Pomona*, put together at the instigation of the Woolhope Club by H. G. Bull and R. Hogg, 1876–85.

As we have established that real cyder was made without the addition of water, we can take the specific gravity of the juice of the various cyder varieties as measured by Knight and the *Pomona*'s chemist as a good indication of the strength of the resultant cyder. To guess at the strength of the seventeenth-century varieties, we have to make the assumption that the amount of sugar in the juice did not vary greatly through the life of the variety. This may be untenable, for there is evidence that Redstreak cyder changed considerably, at least in taste, and was no longer held in esteem by the later eighteenth century. It was only after a considerable search that a single tree of the Redstreak was found by the editors of the *Pomona* a century later, and they were unable to determine its specific gravity. However, when measured by Knight, Redstreak juice had a gravity of 1079, which would have given a cyder of just over 11 per cent alcohol, equivalent to a modern white wine. The juice of the Foxwhelp, the Redstreak's rival, had a very similar original gravity, and the Golden Harvey (Brandy Apple) was 1085, equivalent to just over 12 per cent alcohol. Bull and Hogg give the analysis of every cyder variety illustrated by them (forty-seven) but unfortunately the season when the analysis was made was poor and their figures are uniformly below those of Knight, the highest being 1073 for the Forest Styre and 1068 for the Foxwhelp. The average figure for the *Pomona* varieties is 1044.5, equivalent to less than 6 per cent alcohol. However, we do not know what the figure would have been in a good season, nor whether the apples had been heaped up for a month or six weeks as the best cyder practice dictated. On the other hand Thomas Knight was himself a cyderist and followed these practices, and his figures – averaging about 1081 – are probably a better guide to the strength of cyder in the earlier period. Other evidence came from the French cyderists: part of the Woolhope Club's purpose in instigating the *Pomona* was to rejuvenate the decayed practice of cyder making, and new varieties were brought over from Normandy and local cyder was exhibited at a conference in Paris: the French chemists gave 1067–1080 as the range of specific gravity of their best varieties, so that the strongest cyders were some 12 per cent alcohol (similar to the strength of red wine) with about 3 per cent of the sugar unfermented for residual sweetness.

The habit of adding water is the origin of country cider still made in isolated farms and cottages in Herefordshire, at least half of which is water. It is ciderkin or pirkin made with water because that is the traditional method used by those who have made and drunk cider from the seventeenth century; but made now with apples direct from the tree, because the old cyder which demanded the first use of the fruit is no longer known, and the class of people who drank it then are largely gone, or drink wine.

Cyder cellars

One great advantage that the new cyder had over the old, traditional cider (and to some extent over the weaker forms of cider discussed in the preceding section) was that cyder kept well in cask, and a year's supply could be made at a time. It was obviously efficient to keep a team of men at one job until it was complete rather than repeatedly draw them from other pursuits. The centre of brewing or cyder-making was the manor, the farm, or the rectory, and instead of brewing ale or beer every month or fortnight from stocks of grain, cyder making was a yearly event, taking place in October or November, when farm-work was otherwise slack, and when it was often possible to tap the last untouched barrel of last year's cyder. When it became customary for a farm worker's wages to be paid partly in cider (in addition to the requirements of the master of the house and the household) there was an additional necessity for adequate storage space.

The result of this was that in many houses the cellar, normally suitable for the rapid turn-over of small quantities of beer (which does not keep) had to be modified for the intake of the once

A hogshead arrives at a house in Pembridge, Herefordshire, at the turn
of the century

yearly intake of the correspondingly larger quantities of cyder.
The "hogshead", a wine and cyder measure, became more usual
than the "barrel", a beer measure. A Herefordshire hogshead
could be as much as 110 gallons, very much bigger than a barrel
of beer. There are many instances throughout the west and
south of England of cellar door-jambs cut away in the sixteenth
and seventeenth centuries to accept the hogsheads. In many
cases it was a question of building new cellars with particularly
wide doors, or of incorporating cellars in a new building when
otherwise there would have been none. Cyder, like beer and
other drinks, has to be kept cool if it is to be kept at all, and while

small quantities of beer consumed rapidly and repeatedly might survive in an outhouse, cyder demanded a cellar. In many cases a traditional cellar was simply not possible, because the height of the water table was such that such a hole in the ground would fill with water every winter. Still, the demands of cyder were that a cellar be built, and it was therefore necessary to construct it above ground. The Welsh house of Allt-y-Bela is the first dated example (1599) of a house with a cellar on the ground floor because of the high water table.[29] Another is Trevella, 1601.

The older houses of which the cellars or their entrances were modified to accept the cyder hogsheads are generally of the older "regional style", while the newer fashion in architecture, the "renaissance style", involved the construction of built-in cyder cellars, above ground or below, and certainly, at least in the West Country, called into existence by cyder alone. The change-over in architectural fashion dates from roughly 1600. Occasionally the new cyder cellars would be built *outside* the main house (perhaps because of difficulties with the water table) but sometimes nevertheless in communication with the hall of the house. It became the habit, later in the seventeenth and in the eighteenth century, to build a quite separate "cyder-house", containing all that was necessary for the production of cyder, storage space, the mill, the press, cellar and perhaps loft.[30] By the early seventeenth century cyder cellars were being incorporated as an integral part of the original design, a change that reflects the great increase in the production of cyder and the growth of physical accommodation for it. An example of the integral cyder cellar is found in the farm Greater Woodend, near Dymock, in Gloucestershire.[31]

The cyder industry

We have looked briefly in the preceding sections at the long and persistent history of cider, and the rise and rapid decline of cyder. There are many causes of that decline, interesting in themselves, and which illuminate the people and conditions of the time.

We have already seen that in the Middle Ages cyder was a valuable commodity and was used to make payments in kind for tithes and rents. We also saw that the southern, eastern and home counties of England were plentifully supplied with orchards. By the sixteenth century two developments were under way: cyder was being made for sale in increasing quantities, and the West Country was becoming much more important. The beginning of the industry was simply the household selling off what it did not need, and the economic advantages of doing so were soon apparent. A characteristic argument was put forward by John Norden, whose *The Surveiors Dialogue* of 1610 has the surveyor proposing the planting of apple and pear trees in hedgerows. This would furnish the average small farm or *burgain* in Kent or the western counties with something between one and four tuns of cyder and perry, which would supply the family for a year, and sometimes the method "hath made of the overplus twenty nobles, or ten pounds, more or lesse".[32] The emphasis on the fruit-growing areas of Kent and the West reflects the second point made above, that cyder-making was not being developed on the south coast and home counties. The surveyor's companion is a bailey, and he knew the old apple and pear orchards of the home counties and the unwillingness of the farmers to replace the ancient trees. Perry pear trees are very long lived, and if those known to the bailey were already "very ancient" by 1610, they were probably planted in the fifteenth century. These old orchards, then, were the remains of the medieval cyder habit of central and south England; and as the trees grew old, so the husbandmen lost the art of making cyder, as the bailey makes plain. The surveyor has an economic reason for this, supposing that the proximity of the home counties to London made it more profitable for the apples and pears to be sent for sale direct to the capital than to make cyder and perry from them. Real cyder fruit and perry pears cannot be eaten because of their astringent taste, and so it seems the farmers of the home counties had a second reason to neglect their old trees and concentrate on the production of table-fruit. When they did make cider, the surveyor implies, the farmers of the home counties used apples that served also as table fruit, no doubt in years when supply exceeded demand: the result could not have been real cyder.

These conditions did not apply in the other fruit-growing areas. Kent, although close to the capital, still produced cyder as a result of special attention having been given to the planting of orchards by Henry VIII's fruiterer, Harris. More important, the West Country preserved a knowledge of cyder making and was not given over to the production of table fruit. The most probable reason for this was the distance to London: shipping the fruit to the capital would have been very expensive, and it would hardly have been in good condition when it arrived. Instead the western counties used real cyder fruit to produce a commodity the value of which made the costs of shipping comparatively small, and the stability of which ensured its arrival in good condition. By the later seventeenth century Herefordshire cyder was being shipped to London in bottles, which must have improved its keeping qualities. The herbalist Parkinson speaks of the large quantities of cyder being made at the time in the West Country, and of the difference between cyder- and table-fruit. Much the same is reported by the other great botanist, Gerarde, in his *Historie of Plantes* of 1597, from whom we also hear of a Roger Bodnome (of Bodenham?) who cultivated many varieties of trees for cyder just outside Hereford, whose servants drank nothing but cyder and whose parson's tithes were paid in hogsheads. The progress of cyder making in Herefordshire seems to have been quite sudden, towards the end of the sixteenth century and in the early seventeenth. Camden, whose *Britannia* was published in the early seventeenth century, noted that Herefordshire was remarkable for its wheat and wool, yet Camden's editor in the later part of the century observed that "its present peculiar eminence is in *Fruits* of all sorts, which give them an opportunity of making such vast quantities of *Syder*, as not only to serve their own families (for 'tis their general drink) but also to furnish *London* and other parts of England".[33] That the economy of much of Herefordshire was dependent on the wool trade is seen in the almost perfect preservation of villages like Pembridge, where the prosperity of the late Middle Ages produced

23

buildings that the later decline of the wool trade saved from destruction. The cyder trees were introduced into the Herefordshire economy either by planting in the hedgerows, as Norden suggested, or standing above the wheat that Camden remarked upon. Seventeenth-century cyderists preferred to grow their trees on land used also for rye.

The economics of cyder

One of the chief causes of the decay of cyder was an economic one. Briefly, the cyder "industry" could only be maintained when it remained worth while for the grower to plant new trees. This is not so obvious as it sounds in an industry that was highly fragmented, when a new investment took some seven or ten years to begin bringing in a return and when a mature orchard had a long life. Nevertheless, there was a great deal of discussion among planters in the later seventeenth century. At that time the situation was fairly straightforward: the cyderist would buy land, if he needed it, at perhaps £2 per acre (in Herefordshire) and his trees, including the cost of planting and staking, would cost him a shilling each. Most probably he would plant the most famous of all cyder apples, the Redstreak, a rather small tree that was planted one hundred to the acre, that is, £5. His total investment of some £7 or £8 produced after about seven years about a bushel of apples per tree, rising rapidly to a maximum of three or four bushels.[34] A bushel is a dry volume measure of eight gallons, and so our cyderist's acre would yield him some 3,000 gallons of apples, or between fifteen and twenty hogsheads of cyder to the acre. He would normally press and ferment the juice himself, but if he sold the fruit he could easily see a return on his total capital outlay in a single year. The finished cyder could be sold for a price that could be as much as three times his original capital outlay.[35]

24

The economics of cyder

So making cyder was a profitable business, and it is not surprising that it attracted the middle men, who handled the product between the producer and consumer. These were the eighteenth-century "cider-men", the dealers of the small towns like Upton or Ledbury, who bought the unfermented juice straight from the press at prices agreed among themselves, at the Hereford October fair, without reference to the producer.

It is clear that there were two kinds of product on the market: what was called "common cider" and a higher-quality product made from named varieties of fruit, a drink we are calling cyder in this book. Common cider was the ancestor of the modern commercial drink, and it had originated in the seventeenth century as described above. The main difference of course was that common cider contained a great deal of water, and this difference was heightened by the introduction of the cider dealers into the industry. The apple grower would in general not sell his apples to the dealers, because he made small cider or pirkin from the fruit that had been pressed once to produce the juice sold to the dealers, and in this way a weak cider continued as the standard drink among the ordinary people. Also, when they bought "common cider" by the pint or by the hogshead, it was the mixed juice of various kinds of apple, well watered and probably adulterated in other ways by the dealers.

Cyder continued to be made for the discerning palate and the deep pocket. The economics of the cider trade reveal not only the sharp difference between cider and cyder but also the profits made by the dealers. For example in 1784 there was a good crop of apples and the price of common cider fruit ranged from one-and-six to two shillings for four bushels, that is, not more than it had been a century before. (The average range for the early eighteenth century was two to four shillings.) In the same year the dealers fixed their purchasing price of common cider at fourteen shillings a hogshead. To a certain extent the dealers' prices were dependent on availability, and after an early frost in 1784 the price rose to twenty-five shillings; two years later it reached a peak of five guineas, but was down again to sixteen shillings in 1788. The dealers' selling price for common cider during the same period varied from twenty-five to forty-two shillings, nearly double what they had paid. At Ecford Leigh, near Plympton in Devon, common cider was sold to the dealer at ten shillings a hogshead and re-sold at anything between £2 and £6.[36] (In general perry was cheaper at all levels than cider, and half a guinea would buy a hogshead for consumption.) So the grower sold his juice for an average of less than £1 per hogshead, and out of this he had to meet the costs of picking, carrying, grinding and pressing, which could amount to five shillings a hogshead. If he did not use his own mill, he could use one let out to the public at the rate of perhaps a shilling a hogshead, like the mill at Ross. If he did not have a horse and could not borrow one, then he was obliged to spend more money at another mill: the mill at Newnham charged three shillings for a day's grinding, including the hire of the horse. In a plentiful year the profit shown by the grower would be as little as ten shillings a hogshead, for which he could buy only about twenty, and sometimes as little as ten, pints of good cyder at the local inn. (Imported wine was slightly cheaper.) If the grower rented his house and orchard then half his profit would be absorbed in the rent.[37]

In other words, the making of common cider was becoming less profitable, and this pressure on the growers eventually led to the decay of the cider industry. By the end of the eighteenth century it cost as much as two shillings to buy, plant and stake a cyder-apple tree and it grew increasingly difficult to finance new orchards, or replacement in old, out of profits. This is the critical condition for the continuation of the industry, mentioned at the beginning of this section.

Nor could capital investment have been encouraged by the wildly fluctuating wholesale price of cider, determined by the size of the crop. During the period of twenty-five years from 1769 to 1793 the price of a hogshead of 110 gallons varied between £1 and £5 so erratically that no meaningful average can be reconstructed. Orchards were neglected and little provision made for future crops. In the early years of the nineteenth century, Sir John Sinclair[38] thought that only in a good season would the produce of a cottager's orchard pay his rent, and that it was a difficult question whether the large farmer would find it worth while to establish an orchard. Sinclair calculated that it would cost £320 to establish an orchard of twenty acres, including the mill and interest on the capital spent on planting, that is, £80 or about 2/- per tree, which were standards at forty to the acre. A full crop was not to be expected for about twenty years, according to Sinclair, and meanwhile no profit was to be expected from an undercrop, for ploughing below the trees was not recommended. To calculate the profit arising from the orchard, Sinclair takes a price of rather less than £2 per hogshead, which is hardly

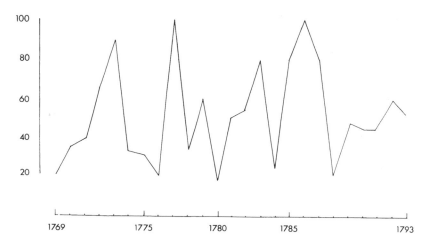

The wholesale price of common cider in shillings per hogshead of 110 gallons, from 1769 to 1793

an improvement on mid-eighteenth century prices; his yield, at 800 gallons to the acre is roughly a half of what Worlidge claimed for the dwarf and prolific Redstreak in the seventeenth century.

Significantly, Sinclair adds that it was more than twice as profitable to grow apples for the table if the farmer lived near a canal or navigable river. We have already seen that it was the convenience of selling table fruit to London that caused the disappearance of cyder from the home counties, and we may suppose that the improved roads and new canals of the eighteenth century opened up many a rural area to trade with the urban centres, making table fruit more profitable.

In contrast, real cyder in the eighteenth century commanded much higher prices. Old Styre fruit fetched three times the price of common cider apples, and Old Styre cyder ranged in price (for

27

consumption) from five to fifteen guineas, about the same as imported wine. Exceptional cyder realized exceptional prices: the Bellamy whose grandfather had raised the Hagloe crab in Hagloe, Gloucestershire, by 1718, was offered sixty guineas for a hogshead of Hagloe cyder at the end of the eighteenth century. Perry from the Squash pear was normally sold for five guineas but in a bad year could rise to twelve guineas, even direct from the press.

Another insight into the economics of cyder and cider is provided by looking at the quantities produced. Figures from the end of the seventeenth and the end of the eighteeenth century suggest that the *same* number of hogsheads, between fifteen and twenty, were being produced from each acre.[39] But other evidence shows that during this period the hogshead almost *doubled in size*. It was a measure perhaps unique to the cyder industry, and its size varied from place to place, no doubt because it had been in use before the industry became established and standardization became desirable. As cyder keeps a good deal better than beer or ale, it was probably found convenient to store it in larger vessels, and we may have one reason for the gradual increase in size. Another reason was the new larger vessel was also used to store cider, which was about double the volume of cyder (from a fixed weight of fruit) by reason of the *added water*. The seventeenth-century cyder hogshead was something over sixty gallons: 63 in Bedfordshire, and 64 in Herefordshire, but by the end of the next century dealers were deciding the price of common cider by the hogshead of 110 gallons.[40] The seventeenth-century hogshead was filled from 30 bushels of apples when making the strongest cyder, while the larger nineteenth-century hogshead was filled by as little as 24 bushels.[41]

The transport of large quantities of cyder from place to place was well under way in the seventeenth century as the cyder industry developed. The main areas of production were Herefordshire and Devon, and the principal market was London; there was a regular sea route from the West Country to Southwark, where Cotton's, Chamberlain's, and Beal's wharves were well-known landing points for cyder. Young trees for planting could also be bought and sold among the growing areas by means of the sea routes, and for the safe transport of trees, Ellis in the eighteenth century recommended one Stephen Tutt, the master of a coaster that plied between Stanton's wharf, Southwark, and various parts of the West Country. Defoe remarked upon the size of the trade when visiting Devon in the early eighteenth century. Cyder became a fashionable drink, most probably because of the peculiar excellence of the Herefordshire Redstreak, a variety of apple developed in the previous century. Worlidge observed the "Gentry and Yeomanry" of the north of England preferred Herefordshire cyder to French wines,[42] and we read that in 1739 Lord Egmont, Stephen Hales and other trustees of the Colony of Georgia were in the habit of drinking at the Cider House, a fashionable resort in London.[43]

Cider as wages

The dealers of the eighteenth century not only diluted the juice to make common cider, but adulterated it to attempt to restore the qualities it had lost in dilution. An early nineteenth-century Worcestershire observer wrote of contemporary cider:

> That produced in the London Taverns ... bears so little affinity to prime cider and perry, that, when tasted by a person conversant in these, it appears no other thing than a whirligig composition of such vapouring elements as he can never hope to reconcile or compose. He smiles at the admiration of the company as they quaff this huffy, frisky, hop, skip, harlequin potation as he witnesses its ludicrous effects upon eyes and noses. The prime ciders of his own county provoke no such titillations. They are quiet, rich, sterling and stomachic; full of fine flavour and strength. They are, in brief, Wine.[44]

This author was writing during the Napoleonic Wars, and like others before him was exhorting his countrymen to produce their own wine and so reduce the import of foreign and particularly French wine. He was of course referring to the cyder of gentlemen, and not to the common cider of the labourer. But he was writing when both cyder and cider were past their peak: within a few years the war was over, and cyder suffered by the fresh importation of French wines, and slowly the habit of paying wages in cider began to disappear. Even by the time Marshall published his *Rural Economy of Gloucestershire* in 1788 the decay of the means of cider production was already evident. All the old fruits, he said, were lost or declining and few trees remained of the Redstreak. The Styre apple was coming to the end of its biological life, as was the Squash pear. Although at the end of the century new markets seemed to be opening up, for apart from supplying London and Bristol, Herefordshire now sent bottled cyder to Ireland and the East and West Indies, yet the rise in the price of wheat and grain in the French wars meant that the old orchards were not replaced as farmers gave their resources to livestock and grain.

But while the old orchards remained, cider continued to be given to farm servants as part of their wages. The difference between the old wine-strength cyder and common cider is well illustrated by Thomas Knight, writing of the making of cyder with all the new-fangled chemistry of the early nineteenth century: "In making cider for the common use of the farmhouse, few of the foregoing rules are, or ought to be, attended to. The flavour of the liquor is here a secondary consideration with the farmer; whose first object must be to obtain a large quantity at small expense."[45]

Indeed the payment of wages in common cider gives us another interesting glimpse of the value of the drink, and of its strength in relation to the fine cyders of the upper classes. In 1794, when good cyder might cost 6d. or a shilling a pint, the Worcestershire labourer was paid a shilling for a day's work of twelve hours, on top of which he was allowed two gallons of cider, perry or beer.[46] If he chose, he could refuse the drink and take home a further twopence in its place. This means that as a wage, common cider was worth only a penny a gallon, although no doubt this low notional price reflects the convenience of the arrangement for employer and employee – who at harvest could drink as much as he liked.

By 1807 Worcestershire wages seem to have doubled, although the real increase, in relation to the cost of provisions, was about 20 per cent. There are records of two shillings being paid if beer or cider was taken in addition; without the drink, two-and-six, or with food in addition, one-and-six. Small beer was then valued at sixpence a gallon, and no doubt one or two gallons were normally taken as wages. Common cider was roughly equivalent in strength and value; women and children were allowed less, perhaps a quart of cider a day.[47]

It is clear, then, that by the end of the eighteenth century, cider was predominantly a working-class drink, and that real cyder was rapidly disappearing as the taste of the upper classes turned towards wine.

> In my own remembrance, wine was seldom produced, but at superior tables, and then only occasionally. The principal gentlemen of the county rivalled each other in their cyders: but now, the case is altered; and cyder, and perry, are seldom produced but at dinner, and then only for a draught, as small beer [i.e. watered cyder]: after the cloth is taken away you must treat with foreign wines, or incur the imputation of not making your friends welcome.[48]

The result was that orchards were often neglected. When the Board of Agriculture commissioned reports on the state of agriculture in the counties of England towards the end of the eighteenth century, they found that cyder fruit was no longer the important crop it had been. The orchards were suffered to remain while they needed no attention and still served to provide the labourers with their gallon a day; but the old varieties were losing their vigour and becoming diseased. Some attempt was made to introduce new varieties from Normandy, but without much success. Moreover, since cider was increasingly identified with the working class, it became easy to disapprove of it and the orchards that produced it, some moralists "alledging, that plenty of cyder is the forerunner of idleness,

31

drunkenness and debauchery. . . ."[49] Indeed, those who reported to the Board from the various counties often adopted a rather high moral tone when quizzing the locals on their handling of their land and orchards. Clark's insistent questions about the wealth of mistletoe on the cyder trees of Herefordshire and their associated decay were obviously resented. "Cannot do everything at once" was the only answer he could get.

Having lost interest in cider, the yeomen and gentry often resented the time lost in making it. Marshall records the following conversation from a Herefordshire farm at the end of the eighteenth century:

"Master, what horse shall I take to drive cider mill?"

"D--n the cider and the mill too; you waste one-half of your time in making cider, and the other half in drinking it."

Very similar sentiments were expressed more than a century later, when the practice of supplying free cider to the labourers was all but dead: a Herefordshire farmer was asked why he had stopped making cider in the early 1920s: "Well, I paid 'em to make it, and I paid 'em to drink it, and still the buggers weren't satisfied. So I stopped making it."[50]

It was only very occasionally that interest in real cyder lingered. One example was William Symonds, an ancestor of the present Bill Symonds, the Stoke Lacy cyderist, who was busy at the end of the eighteenth century making a range of cyders. He is reported by Marshall to have made a hogshead of cyder solely from the skins and cores of the fruit, where it was thought all the flavour lay. The result was a strong and high-flavoured cyder, while that made from the remaining flesh of the apple was insipid.

The part-payment of wages in cider was part of a more general practice of payment in kind, including food, free lodging, and use of land. At its best, the system worked to the advantage of both parties, for the labourer had the goods cheaper than he could buy them and the producer was saved the trouble of realizing actual cash in a sale at probably low wholesale prices; this must have been a considerable advantage in the case of cider when the price fluctuated wildly from year to year. But in the second half of the nineteenth century the practice of paying wages partly in cider began to diminish. In one example in 1872 sixpence more was given for every gallon of cider withdrawn from wages.[51] In the 1880s the temperance movement appears to have had some influence in replacing cider with a cash payment (in some cases free tea was supplied instead!),[52] and it was probably in the government's interest to encourage the payment of wages in cash rather than perquisites, "perks", in kind. The

Making cider in the 1920s: the watered juice is being poured into a hogshead through a tundish

problem was dealt with in a series of "Truck Acts" up until the end of the century, in which the regulation of the employers' "truck shops" were promulgated. These shops were those from which the payments in kind were made and in which the labourers were expected to spend their sometimes nominally cash wages. In the case of agricultural workers it was recognized that some forms of payment in kind were proper – food, non-alcoholic drink, accommodation – but payment in cider was discouraged, and soon died out. The loss was regretted, at least by the labourers.

This was one of the principal reasons for the decline of cider. The farmer and gentleman had no need to make common cider for his labourers, and from choice he himself drank wine or brandy, forgetting the cyder that earlier moralists, prelates, patriots and economists had urged his father and grandfather to make.

Excise duty

A good indication of the size of the cider industry in the eighteenth century is the fact that the government proposed to raise revenue by taxing the sale of cider and perry. In 1763 Lord Bute, the prime minister, forced through a Bill to impose ten shillings duty on each hogshead, payable by the first purchaser. This was not the first tax on cider, for excise duty had been imposed in 1643;[53] this cannot have been collected systematically, and one of the rare references to it is made by Ellis in 1754, who mentions a tax of seven shillings per hogshead, payable to the Crown.[54] The new duty was therefore technically an increase of three or four shillings for the *sale* of cider, while members of the family drinking cider made for them at home each paid five shillings, the cider being untaxed.

The tax aroused great opposition, both during the progress of the Bill and after the publication of the Act. The industry had been developing under William III and Queen Anne partly because of the exclusion of French wines during the continental wars, and the new tax was resented by those who sold cider profitably to London and elsewhere, by those who paid their labourers with it, by those who thought it preferable to French wine, for patriotic and economic reasons, and by those who made

"The Scotch Yoke"

cyder for their own consumption. This last group secured the first concession in an Act which reduced the family's own contribution from five shillings to two shillings per head, but this made little difference to the opposition to the tax. Bute was burnt in effigy, lampoons and broadsheets[55] issued from the presses, and committees of nobility, gentry, clergy and farmers were formed in Worcester, Hereford and Gloucester to seek a repeal of the Act. Bute was represented as a Scot imposing on the native English a yoke comparable to the "Norman yoke" upon the Saxons:

Of *Freedom* no longer, let Englishmen boast,
Nor *Liberty* more be their favourite Toast;
The *Hydra* OPPRESSION your *Charter* defies,
And galls *English* necks with the *Yoke* of EXCISE.

In vain you have conquer'd, my brave Hearts of Oak,
Your *Lawrels*, your *Conquests*, are all but a *Joke;*
Let a r-s-ly PEACE serve to open your Eyes,
And the d--n--ble Scheme of a CYDER-EXCISE.

I appeal to the Fox, or his Friend JOHN A BOOT,
If tax'd thus the *Juice*, then how soon may the *Fruit?*
Adieu then to good *Apple-puddings* and *Pyes*,
If e'er they should taste of a cursed EXCISE.

The illustration accompanying "The Scotch Yoke" shows the burning of Bute's effigy, which holds "Peace" in one hand and "Excise upon Cyder" in the other.

Cyder-making equipment

Where real cyder is to be made, the juice must be efficiently extracted from the apple. We have seen that the earliest cider was made by crude extraction techniques involving the use of water, and even at the height of English cyder-making, the poorer country people, who had neither horse nor mill, crushed their apples by hand. In Devon as late as the eighteenth century apples were beaten in a wooden trough made from a hollowed trunk of a tree, in which two men armed with long-handled beatles (hammers) were said to be able to crush twenty or thirty bushels of apples during the course of a day. Even such a trough or "pound" was a luxury for others, who were obliged to crush the fruit in a tub with a rolling pin.[56]

Cyder-making equipment

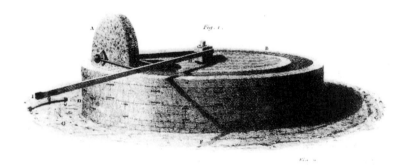

Above A small stone mill and a verjuice press, 1747
Below A horse-mill of the traditional pattern but with the trough composed of some twenty stones, rather than the two of its simple seventeenth-century ancestor. Before the introduction of mechanical sources of power in the nineteenth century, the traditional horse-mill and hand-press greatly increased in size in order to cope with the volume of production

The cyder mill that survives in farms and cottages in the West Country today is a form of the "edge-runner" mill, a heavy stone wheel running round a central post in a trough. It is a heavy piece of equipment and was expensive to install, and was called into existence only by the profitable cyder industry. The mill was made of local stone wherever possible, to save the cost of carriage, and most Herefordshire mills are made of Old Red Sand-

37

stone; those of the Channel Islands are granite. Although the materials were local, the design was the same in all cases, differing only in the number of parts composing the base of the mill, in which the trough is cut: small mills are constructed by two semicircular halves, while large mills of farms and great houses may be composed of four or five.[57] The design of the mill is of great interest. It was not a case of the local workmen considering the best way of crushing apples and fortuitously coming up with the same answer all over the country; all mills were copied from others already in existence, and these in turn from older examples. There was in other words a traditional pattern of what a cyder mill should be. But most mills in England are seventeenth

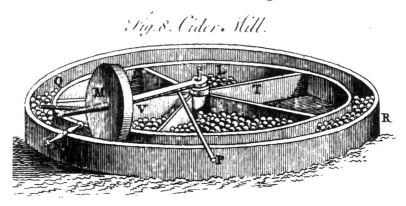

Fig. 8. Cider. Mill.

The parts of a mill: R is the chase around which is pulled the runner, M, by the horse harnessed at N. Fruit is stored in the spaces L and T, and in the chase at Q is to be reduced to pummice or murc by the action of the runner

century and later, and none are likely to be older than the later sixteenth, so it is evident that the making of mills, like the cyder habit itself, was imported from elsewhere. The answer is that it came from France, perhaps via the Channel Islands; but this was only the last stage in a series of borrowings from other countries and cultures: in fact the West Country cyder mill, now so often forgotten in some dark corner of an ancient farm building, is the direct descendant of the mills used in antiquity in the lands of the Near East and Mediterranean for preparing olives for the extraction of oil.

In tracing back the history of the cyder mill, we may note that edge-runner mills in general have been used for a variety of purposes and the design was clearly adaptable. There was a great extension of the use of machines in the later Middle Ages and Renaissance, and edge runners were used for olives, woad and other dye-stuffs, linseed, sugar cane, charcoal (for gunpowder) and metallic ores.[58] Cyder mills in Devon resemble mills used as late as the eighteenth century by tanners for grinding bark.[59] Renaissance accounts of contemporary machines describe single-wheel edge runners,[60] sometimes driven by water. French cyder mills sometimes had two rolling wheels,[61] a feature which links them more closely to the ancient olive-oil mill, described below.

The olive mill was known to the Romans as the *mola olearia*, and from the description left by Columella we can see that it had two stone rollers mounted at opposite ends of a common axle pivoted at the centre-post. Two rollers were necessary, one to balance the other, because these wheels were lifted by their bearings from the base of the trough in which they ran, so as not to

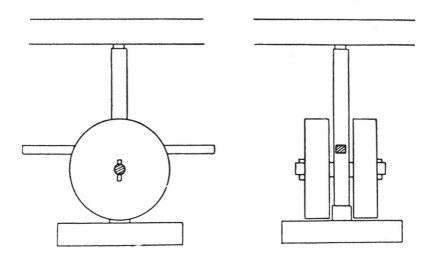

Reconstruction of the *mola olearia* described by Columella. The runners are flat where they touch the base, like those of a cyder mill, but there is no trough. The clearance for the olive stones is maintained by the balance of the second wheel, as in the *trapetum*. First century A.D.

39

crush the olive stones. There is no corresponding need to avoid crushing the pips in apples, so the cyder mill was made more simply with a single wheel, the full weight of which is allowed to fall upon the fruit. (It is true that some cyder mills have two wheels, but the second is a smaller, trailing wheel, following closely behind the first and designed to run over the pulp that tends to be pushed to the periphery of the trough.) Forms of the *mola olearia* still survive in southern Europe. Another form of this mill was the Greek *trapetum*, said by Pliny to have been invented in Athens. It was a smaller mill, designed for human power rather than that of the horse, unlike the *mola olearia* and the cyder mill. The only real difference between these old mills and the cyder mill is the need to suspend and balance the *two* rollers of the olive mill. This may well be a secondary modification of a simpler and more primitive mill with a single roller and no clearance. One particular carving on a classical sarcophagus appears to have only one roller in the mill depicted, and may be such a simple, primitive mill. The result is so surprisingly like a cyder mill of the seventeenth century that one is inclined to wonder whether, as is claimed, the second roller of the mill has been destroyed in the relief.

It is just possible that the sarcophagus mill[62] *was* a cyder mill or a mill to prepare soft fruits like oranges for the extraction of juice. If it *did* only have one runner then it could not have been an olive mill, for the single heavy wheel would be hopelessly out of balance and would soon wear its bearing and lose the clearance necessary to preserve the olive stones. Equally, the ordinary *olive* mill could not have been used efficiently to crush apples (and after all both the Greeks and Romans knew of cider) because of the half-inch or so clearance between the roller and the base of the trough. The reason is that the cyder mill does not work by the weight of the roller alone, and those who have used one will know that the roller, weighing at least half a ton, will with surprising ease at first roll over the top of the scarcely broken apples. Any clearance would prevent the grinding of the apples, which depends upon the *twisting* motion between the roller and the bottom surface of the trough. That is to say, the roller is a wheel with a greater diameter on one side than the other, and if left to run freely on a flat surface would describe a large circle.

But it is constrained by the attachment of its axle to the central post and the trough in which it runs to describe a very much smaller circle, round which it always skids. The resulting wear turns the flat bottom of the trough into a rounded groove that fits the now-rounded grinding surface of the roller.

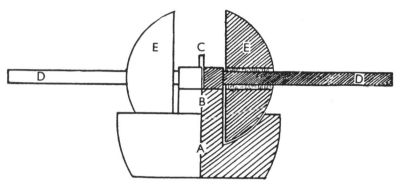

The ancestor of the cyder mill, the Greek *trapetum* used for crushing olives. In order to avoid crushing the olive stones a small clearance was left between the mill runners, *E*, and the circular trough in the base, *A*. Thus the runners were not supported by the floor of the trough as in the cyder mill, and it was desirable to have two runners to achieve balance and reduce wear on the bearing on which the operating beam, *D*, was supported around a central pin, *C*. The runners were about 80 centimetres in diameter

The action of the cyder mill has not always been understood by those who made the mills, and when first made, the rolling surface of the runner was cut with a pattern of grooves very similar to those used locally on the flat circular surface of flour-mill stones. Now, the channels in the flour-mill stone have the obvious purpose of guiding the grain to the grinding surfaces and the flour away, and they have to be recut when worn; but there is no comparable action in the cyder mill and the grooves would have served no purpose. This pattern of grooves is now found only in those mills that were, by some historical accident, never used. As remarked above, cyder mills were not *designed* locally to tackle the problem of crushing apples, but the design was borrowed from a pre-existing model (*all* mills rotate in a clockwise direction) and built from local materials. In this case the builder borrowed his design from two different sources.

The growth of crafts and industries in the Renaissance brought the ancient edge-runner mill into a variety of uses. Here a water-driven edge runner is being used. Note that because its function is to *grind*, a single wheel without clearance has replaced the balanced double wheel of the *mola olearia*

Cyder-making equipment

Above Worlidge's "Ingenio" cyder mill, 1676, designed to replace the traditional stone horse-mill

Below Another version of the "Ingenio". The boy is presumably removing the pummice to carry to the press

43

The traditional stone cyder mill was expensive to install and it required a horse for its operation. In the 1670s Worlidge introduced his "Ingenio", a hand-turned contrivance in which two rollers in a wooden frame did the work of the horse-mill. While the cyder industry was growing and people were loth to go to the trouble and expense of installing a horse-mill, the ingenio had some measure of success. It had the advantages that it could easily be modified to take a belt-drive from a water mill (later versions called "scratters"[63] or "scratchers" are still driven by belts from a tractor), that it was mobile, and that at £3 to £10 it was considerably cheaper than the stone mill, which needed a special room that could be used for nothing else, both of which together might cost £20 to £30. Worlidge claimed that his ingenio would grind three times the amount of apples as the horse mill in a given time, and that the quality of the juice was superior because the ingenio did not grind the pips. The ingenios were made by Henry Allen in Exeter Street, near the Strand, and sent about the country; to some extent Worlidge's publications are advertising copy for his mill. However, it is difficult to say how many were sold, and the wooden frame proved less durable than the simple stone mill, and few ingenios survive.[64]

Cyder, science and society

The quantity and quality of the cyder made in the seventeenth century drew the attention of various groups of people who were thinking about the large-scale problems of the society in which they lived. In looking for the origins of cyder and cider, we are struck by the economic and political problems of importing large quantities of foreign wines: cyder was seen as a native substitute for wine,[65] lessening the dependence upon foreign and potentially hostile nations abroad and diverting currency to profitable home-based industries. No doubt this wine-substitute

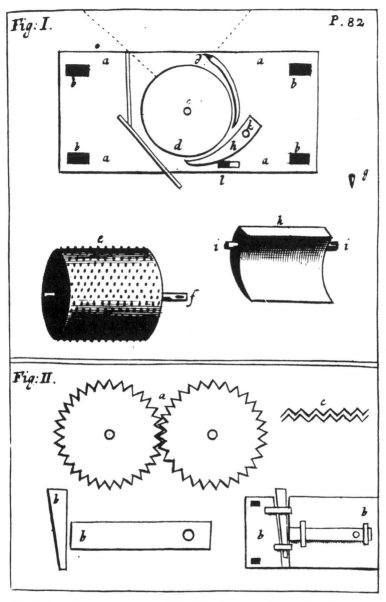

Fig: I.

Fig: II.

The internal arrangements of Worlidge's new mill, notably the grinding cylinder *e*. The axle, *f*, of the cylinder rests upon brass bearings, *c*, located in the wooden frame, *a*. The cylinder, of oak or beech, is studded with iron pegs that break up the fruit, which is guided to it by a convex plate, *h*, the hinge pegs of which are also located in the wooden frame, *i* and *k*. This plate is adjustable, being moved by a transom located in the mortise *l*. The dotted lines indicate the position of the hopper had the strength and something of the palate of wine; but we also hear the economic argument that cultivation of a domestic cider habit would reduce the use of grain in brewing beer, thus making more grain available for the production of bread. Perhaps beer or ale-strength cider was in the minds of the agrarian reformers, as a natural substitute for the long drink of those who did not normally drink wine.

The people who were thinking about these problems were also concerned with the intellectual and scientific progress of the age. The Renaissance had generally done much to restore the Greek and Hellenistic view that man and the natural world were worthy of study (and were not, as believed in the Middle Ages, to be ignored as partners in the Fall from Paradise). The Renaissance put an interpretation on this study that was more theological than that of the "pagan" Greeks: man was made in the image of God, and was a microcosm of God's creation at large, the natural world; in creating both, God had used divine Reason, some of which was possessed also by man: it followed that to a certain extent at least, man could follow and appreciate that reason by examining the natural world. Natural philosophy, the science of the seventeenth century, became a pious exercise, and "the wisdom and goodness of God in the Creation" was proclaimed from innumerable seventeenth-century pulpits backed up with a display of natural-historical and scientific knowledge.

This view took a particular turn with the Puritans of the early part of the century. Their view of history proclaimed to them that the space of a comparatively few years would bring in the beginning of the Millennium, when for a thousand years the reign of Christ on earth would bring unparalleled benefit to mankind. The preparations for this were urgent, and moulded men's views. Reform of most earthly institutions was necessary; nothing less than revolution would make due preparation. Among the principal aims to be achieved by revolution of education, of science, and of learning, was the restoration of man to the state of divine grace he had enjoyed before the Fall. Had not Adam named the animals and plants? Did not that indicate that he had innate knowledge of their properties and powers? A knowledge that had been lost at the Fall? It was true that by seeking improperly after knowledge Adam had brought disgrace upon himself, but the Puritans believed that by limiting their enquiry into science to *secondary* causes, that is, those not related directly to the inscrutable power of God, they could restore to man that knowledge of, and command over, the natural world that he had possessed in paradise. Perhaps chief among the propagandists' topics of the time was the topic of the reform of husbandry and agriculture at large.[66] They took their text from the philosophy of Bacon, who had emphasized the secondary causes of nature, and had avoided questioning the

A hand-operated mill of the early nineteenth century. Although obviously related both to the earlier "Ingenio" of Worlidge and the later scratters, the shape of the grinding rollers is notably distinct. The rollers seem designed to engage the apples emerging from the hopper without the need for further apparatus; this does without some of the complexities of Worlidge's "Ingenio", but seems not to have been entirely satisfactory, for later devices returned to the studded cylindrical roller, on to which the apples were forced by the action of a piston metaphysical first cause, by stating that the aims of science should be directed towards action and use, the understanding and *controlling* of nature to the benefit of man. (We shall hear below of Bacon's remarks on cider and his advice to plant fruit trees.) This struck another chord in the Puritans' minds. Eden had been a fruitful garden, and Adam before the Fall had not been idle, but had laboured as a good husbandman. Such fruitfulness could be generated within the Commonwealth to the benefit of the entire nation.

The establishment of the new learning could only be achieved by improving communications between those taking part, so, groups of reformers, philosophers and scientists met and corresponded on the practical details of instituting reformed husbandry. These groups were like that which matured into the Royal Society at the Restoration. They were motivated by a variety of political and religious views, but they shared a common view of the practicality of science, and they shared an inspiration from Bacon. He had pointed to the discoveries that were resulting from the new voyages of discovery, heralding the beginning of a growth of knowledge that would grow into the Great Instauration of knowledge. The old, inherited knowledge would no longer suffice for new conditions; new remedies were to be sought for the new diseases of the age, whether brought about by new adventures (we shall discover below the Baconian use of cider on long voyages) or by the widely accepted idea of the degeneration of man. Such men as John Beale and Sir Paul Neile, both of whom wrote on cider, were associated with Hartlibb and others in these early meetings of scientists and reformers.

Social reform was seen as one of the major avenues to prepare for the coming of the millennium. It was suggested that landowners should be legally obliged to plant a certain proportion of their land with fruit trees. R. Austen, who wrote a *Treatise on Fruit Trees* in 1653 (it included "The Spiritual use of an Orchard"), approached Cromwell with an appeal for state aid in a national scheme for the planting of fruit trees. The appeal was unsuccessful, but it embodied many of the points that were to be used many times again: the planting of fruit trees in hedges and orchards would supply timber, both for joiners and heavy use;

the bark would supply the tanner's needs, which were currently raising the price of leather to a very high level; wood useless for construction would provide fuel; the general adoption of cider instead of ale would save malt, the wood used in preparing the malt (as fuel), and the grain itself, freeing land for other purposes; moreover, cider was such a health-giving drink that Englishmen, newly prosperous from following the above advice, "would be a strong and healthy People, and Long-lived, able to goe forth to Warre and bee a terror to all our Enemies".[67]

This is the background to the seventeenth-century discussions on the nature and the value of cyder in the Royal Society and elsewhere. Evelyn's *Pomona* is an invaluable source for these discussions; the book itself was an appendix to a larger work, the *Sylva*, a treatise on trees and their use in the national economy, prepared for the Royal Society.[68] *Pomona* is not merely a cyderist's guide, but has the high ideals of a spokesman of the new horticulture, and tells us much about cyder and cider. When Evelyn, in a happy phrase, spoke of "Our Design of relieving the want of *Wine*, by a succedaneum of *Cider* (as lately improv'd) . . ." he was referring to Redstreak cyder of Herefordshire, made and drunk as a wine. A London vintner travelling through Herefordshire at the time (about 1676) was challenged by a well-known local cyderist to produce a Spanish or French wine better than Redstreak cyder; he accepted, but many times failed, before a panel of judges. Another of Evelyn's stories concerns the perry of the Turgovian pear, which had travelled eight hundred miles with a member of the Royal Society[69] and with which Evelyn entertained a distinguished company at his home, Sayes Court, near Deptford: all, including Sir Kenelm Digby (who had his own ideas on cider)[70] were "surpriz'd with the richness of the Liquor". The circumstances suggest that this was a wine-strength perry, matured and portable in small bottles. French wine was the natural standard of comparison for cyder and perry, and West Country cyderists were not slow to proclaim the superiority of their products. Beale describes a mixture of the juice of the Imny-Winter pear and that of crab apples as better than French wine (although the raw pear was uneatable: "It purgeth more violently than a Galenist").[71]

The *practical* nature of the Royal Society's interest in cyder is revealed not only by the attempts to replace wine but by an active search for new varieties of fruit and by experimentation with techniques of production. Beale's description of the Imny-Winter perry is directed partly at a Dr Pell, who seems to have been a British diplomat at Zurich, and who was also concerned with bringing the Turgovian pear to Evelyn's notice.

Wine-strength cyder as a substitute for imported wines was quite different from the weaker water ciders and small ciders discussed above, which were the equivalent of ale or beer. It was also possible to contrive a substitute for brandy by distilling cyder. Worlidge in the *Vinetum Britannicum* was, like Evelyn, alive to the economic and other advantages of drinking cyder instead of imported wine, and the argument applied equally to

A cyder mill devised by Robert Hooke, the Curator of the Royal Society and contemporary of Evelyn. It was designed to prevent the solid parts of the apple descending with the juice – that is, it acted like a press as well as a mill

imported brandy; Worlidge recommends the distillation of cyder. The argument was also taken up energetically by Richard Haines,[72] who proposed the making of "Cyder-Royal" by distillation, "For the Good of those Kingdoms and Nations That are Beholden to Others, and Pay Dear for WINE". Haines's starting point was *common* cider, at thirty shillings a hogshead, and his purpose was to increase its strength to and beyond that of wine. If the practice were widely adopted by the northern European countries, Haines foresaw a reduction of price of wine produced in the South as well as other advantages, and he secured a patent from the king. Haines and his partners claimed twenty-one shillings and sixpence per annum from those who would sell the product, and the same amount from any member of the public who wished to make cyder-royal for his own use, the licence extending over fourteen years. The technique was simply to double distill one hogshead of cider and add the result to a second hogshead: this, said Haines, produced a liquor as strong as French wine, with a value of a shilling a quart, from materials costing threepence. Every gallon of cider produced about a pint of spirit in this manner, and Haines argued that a pint and a half of spirit should be added to the gallon of common cider to make it as strong as Spanish or Canary wine. Haines was in fact producing a fortified wine, in the same way as sherry, Madeira and port were made by the addition of brandy (which Haines also used).

Although there are later references[73] to the distillation of cyder in England, the habit did not catch on, and there is no tradition of a home-produced calvados like that of France.[74]

Cyder and medicine

When cyder became well known in sixteenth-century England, it was natural that its effects on the human body should be

51

explained in terms of the medicine of the time. During the three centuries or so of the popularity of real cyder, two important medical facts were discovered: when made with certain equipment, it produced lead-poisoning in the drinker, and, when drunk on long voyages at sea, it cured scurvy. Long experience preceded both these discoveries, and we cannot always tell whether the early accounts of the medical virtues of cyder contain empirical inklings of this knowledge, or were simply concerned to explain the good and bad effects respectively of moderate and excessive drinking of cyder. We can, however, continue to look for evidence of the difference between cider and cyder.

To understand this evidence, we must first understand something of the medical theory of the time. Cyder came to England at the same time as the Renaissance of the arts and the sciences; and renaissance medicine of the most approved sort was that of the Greeks, and was a millennium and a half old. The spokesman of Greek medicine was Galen, the Greek physician of Marcus Aurelius and Commodus. Galen was also a philosopher and, we may suppose, something of a viticulturist, for he had inherited but a sharp tongue from his mother, and a vineyard from his father. Galen's entire physiological scheme revolved around the image of wine fermenting in the vat, and we can see how naturally notions about the medical virtues of cyder fell into this analogy in the Renaissance. Food taken into the stomach could be compared, in Galen's analogy, with the whole grapes, which need preparation before the substantive juice can be expressed. These preparations over, the still raw and unconcocted food was passed to the liver, where (said Galen) the fundamental physiological change took place, converting the food-juice into blood. The process was one of refining, like fermentation, and the first by-product was a light, frothy "superfluity" which rose from the liver to be collected in the gall bladder: this was yellow bile, or choler. Its analogue in fermentation was the semi-solid froth on top of the wine or the "floating feculancies" which cyder throws off in the first days of fermentation. The purification continued with the depositing of a heavy "superfluity" from the new blood. This was black bile or (from the Greek) melancholy, which was collected into the spleen. Its analogue is the dark lees of the wine, left behind in the vat when the wine is racked off into a fresh vessel. In Galen's scheme, both black and yellow bile were excrements, to be voided from the body; yet while in the body they could, in excess, produce illness, so that a *choleric* person and a *melancholic* person suffered symptoms that we still associate with these terms.

But yellow and black bile were only two of the four cardinal humours of the body. The other two were blood, the end product of the bodily "fermentation", and phlegm, thought to be produced in the brain. Health was a balance of all four humours, and disease imbalance, one or more of the humours being present in excess. Persons with too much blood were plethoric or *sanguine*, which does not now have quite the same meaning; and those with an excess of phlegm were of course *phlegmatic*, a term which still carries many of the connotations of the Greek scheme. The English language carries other remnants of this scheme of physiology, and the term "temper" or "temperament" ultimately refers to balance of the humours upon which health depends. Likewise "complexion" referred to the fundamental nature of the tissues of the body as envisaged by the Greeks.

This introduces one other topic whose acquaintance we must make in order to understand the part that cyder was thought to play in renaissance medicine. Each of the four humours, blood, yellow bile, black bile and phlegm, had a pair of qualities. There were four Qualities, hot, cold, moist and dry, and they were the fundamental characteristics of everything material that made up the universe. In particular the four material elements of the universe, earth, air, fire and water, each had a pair of Qualities, as did the four humours of the body, which meant that humours, elements and qualities formed the basis of a rational scheme of the world, both organic and inorganic.

It was not difficult of course for the medical men to set out that the four seasons of the year also had a pair of qualities, so that summer, for example, was hot and dry. It followed that summer was a time of hot and dry diseases, and that, to restore the balance of humours, cold and moist medicines should be taken.

Now we are in a position to appreciate contemporary thinking on the medical virtues of cyder. The physician Andrew Boorde,

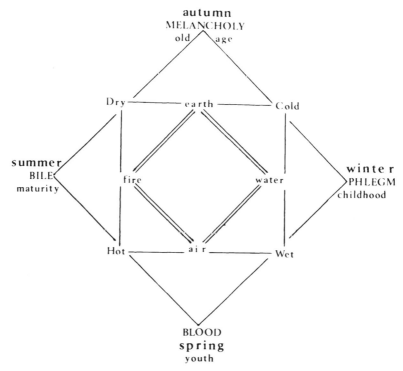

writing in 1542, was not quite sure of the difference between cyder and perry, but confident enough about their medical effects:

> But the beest is not praysed in physicke, for cyder is colde of operacyon, and is full of ventosyte, wherefore it doth ingendre evyll humours, and doth savage too moche the natural heat of man, and doth let digestyon, and doth hurt the stomacke; but they the which be used to it, if it be dronken in harvyst, it doth lytell harm.

In other words, the predominating Quality of cyder was thought to be cold, and its prime effect was to reduce the "innate heat" of the body, the heat, that is, by which the soul or principle of life acted on the body and performed all physiological actions. As we have seen, the prime of these physiological actions was the digestion of food to produce blood, and so it was logical that the coldness of cyder should impair digestion and affect the stomach. Of course, if a man were excessively warm, as he might well be from the work and weather at harvest-time, then cyder was a very appropriate drink. In a similar vein, the "evyll humours" of Boorde are the excessive or perverted humours of standard pathological theory: the whole description is logical in the sense of following a set of rules, and the only points of possible empirical description of the nature and effects of cyder are its coldness and "ventosyte".[75]

So the "coldness" and "wetness" of cyder made it, in sixteenth-century medicine, a natural drink to be taken by those with "hot" and "dry" diseases, such as fevers, or "hot Agues" as William Lawson called them, in advocating the medical consumption of cyder.[76] The rationality of this technique – achieving a healthy balance of humours and qualities in the body by the application of opposites – was extended to the other empirically observed property of cyder, that of "ventosyte", which was almost certainly a description of the purging effect of cyder, and more particularly perry: it loosens the bowels, and then as now has the unwary drinker scuttling incontinently for the privy. This was known as "dissolving the belly" at least as early as the herbalist Gerarde in the sixteenth century. The effect was rationalized into current theory by assuming that the wetness and other qualities of cyder encouraged the expulsion of the dry black bile, which we noted above as an excremental by-product of digestion. As black bile caused the condition of melancholy – gloomy apprehensiveness, inactivity – its removal by cyder was clearly the cause of the drinker becoming cheerful and sprightly, "peart" as they say in Herefordshire. Such an explanation may be found in the works of the great English herbalist of the early seventeenth century, Parkinson.[77] Parkinson also remarks that (not surprisingly) distilled cyder has the same effect. (This is one of the few scraps of evidence of an English practice of distillation of cyder.)

By the time Evelyn was writing in the second half of the seventeenth century, the rigidity of the old ideas was beginning to break down. Evelyn says that cider is a specific medicine against *"that unsociable* Spleen", but he is not thinking simply of its wet and cold qualities in the old-fashioned sense, for he is also using "bile" and "spleen" much more in the modern sense as synonyms of "anger"[78] or lowness of spirits. Indeed, he also says of cider that it is *above all the most eminent, soberly to exhilarate the* Spirits *of us* Hypochondriacal Islanders". By *"soberly to exhilarate the* Spirits" he does not intend a paradox of inebriation without intoxication, but he means that the *spirits* of man are made more vigorous by the powers of cider. According to the traditional account, which Evelyn was still following, man had two sets of spirits: the vital spirits, that existed in the heart, and were responsible for emotions, and animal spirits, which were located in the brain, and which controlled voluntary motion and were responsible to the reasoning soul. It was the "quickness" of cider that moved the spirits more actively, and thus opposed what Evelyn called *hypochondriac* diseases characteristic of Englishmen. By this he does not mean to imply that his countrymen were so many malingerers, but that they suffered from discomforts of the *hypochondre*, or large intestine. Not far below the surface of Evelyn's thinking is the traditional notion that purging removes melancholy and bile.

So the Englishman of the early seventeenth century found that cyder raised his spirits, lowered his temperature and dissolved his belly. He also maintained that under its benign influence he would not contract rheumatism or stone of the bladder, that there was moral but not medical danger in getting drunk upon cyder twice a day and that it was a wonderful preservation in old age.[79] The well-known story of a morris dance at Hereford races in 1609, danced by twelve men with a total of 1200 years, was used to demonstrate the longevity that resulted from cyder-drinking, and Martin Johnson, who became Vicar of Dilwyn in 1651, boasted of the longevity of his parishioners and the excellence of their cyder in a poem of seventy lines.

Vin de Paris, Vin d'Orleans, vin Sharoon
With all the Gallick wines are not so boone
As hearty Sider, y‍ᵗ strong drink of wood
In fullest tydes refines and purges blood,

he sang

attributing the vigour of his centenarian parishioners to their Lenten diet of toast and cyder, which among the younger villagers "heightens their appetites and creates in them a durable strength to labour".[80]

In short cyder, like another drink new to the seventeenth century, coffee, was held to have a range of medical effects, noted by its drinkers and rationalized into current medical theory by the physicians (coffee was held to act upon the animal spirits in a way very like that of cyder).[81] But cyder had one very real medical quality that, although reported early, was never widely adopted and could not be rationalized into medical theory: it cured scurvy.

This was a fact of potentially enormous importance: it is a commonplace of a nautical history that by the eighteenth century scurvy was claiming more lives on board ship than any enemy action. A large ship of the line could carry 800 men, and it was not uncommon for more than half of these to be lost to scurvy during a long voyage. In humanitarian, economic and military terms the loss was immense, and although *some* ship's surgeons had discovered, and published, a cure for scurvy in the early seventeenth century, it was not until the later eighteenth century that the naval authorities finally made arrangements for all sailors to be supplied with fruit juice, thus ending scurvy at a stroke.

When scurvy was first described in the sixteenth century, it was an awkward disease. It did not fit into the classical categories of disease that the Renaissance had made the new medical canon; an anxious search among the ancient authors revealed that the only condition remotely similar was one arising from an obstructed spleen, described by Hippocrates; and it had no pure Greek name, only the ugly Low German *Schorbuk*, hardly dignified by the new Latin *scorbutus*. Perhaps, then, it was a new disease, like the pox, and no doubt also like the pox, was due to the degenerate physical state and moral laxity of modern man. But an alternative solution, soon put forward, was that scurvy was unknown to the classical physicians because they had not strayed far from the Mediterranean, while scurvy was now found to be widespread only among the countries of northern Europe. Indeed, it came to be thought of as a disease as characteristic of Britain as the "hypochondriac" diseases mentioned by Evelyn. Certainly fully half of the cases of disease taken into the new Scottish hospitals of the earlier eighteenth century[82] were cases of scurvy, and up to that time nine authors out of ten who wrote on scurvy[83] were northern European – German, Dutch, Scandinavian and British, with four Frenchmen and a negligible contribution from Italy, which was otherwise in the forefront of medical activity.

So by the late sixteenth and early seventeenth centuries scurvy was recognized as a disease of northern and maritime peoples. In emulation of classical theory, attempts were made to find causes in cold and foggy weather, and it was widely accepted (again there were good classical reasons for doing so) that a poor diet, with many preserved victuals and little fresh fruit and vegetables, was at least partly responsible. Naturally, such causes were held to generate corrupt humours within the body and the effort of therapeutic techniques went into removing them. Although some authors distinguished between "land scurvy" and "sea scurvy" it was also widely accepted that the same disease occurred wherever conditions brought forward the same poor diet, whether on board ship, in camp or under siege. For centuries the poorest peasants of northern Europe must have faced scurvy in the early spring, long after last season's fruit and vegetables had been eaten and while the community lived on salted and dried provisions.

But there was no medieval Germanic Hippocrates to enlighten later ages about scurvy, and sixteenth-century Europe had to discover for itself. It became aware of scurvy in two main ways. First, medical intelligence was now broadcast more readily and cheaply by means of the printed book. Second, commercial and political ventures now forced the crews of large ships to spend much longer on board. The medieval merchantman, through want of size and navigational techniques, had rarely strayed far from the coast, but fifteenth- and sixteenth-century ships were ocean-going. Vasco da Gama is said to have lost a hundred of a complement of 160 men in 1497. English attention was drawn to scurvy at sea almost in a single episode, the first voyage (1605) of a squadron of the newly formed East India Company. Captain James Lancaster commanded the *Dragon* (202 men) and the squadron included the *Hector*, *Susan* and *Ascension* with 223 men between them. Of the total ships' complement 114 were lost to scurvy, but no death occurred on the *Dragon*, because Lancaster had made a supply of lemon juice available to the men.

That should, of course, have been the end of the story, that scurvy had been contained by this discovery. But in fact it was more than a century and a half before a concerted effort in this direction succeeded. This is not the place to go into the reasons for this failure, but it was clearly a failure to get the right information to the right man at the right time, and with all possible emphasis. One of the things that clouded the issue was that lemon juice was only one of hundreds of remedies, and that when lemons were not available there was little to guide the choice of an alternative.

One of these alternatives was cyder. Its antiscorbutic properties were probably known in the sixteenth century when it became a well-known drink; and of course, it had one great advantage over fresh fruit in that it kept a great deal better.

In the voyages of the sixteenth and seventeenth centuries, some cyder seems to have been taken on board in a diluted form, either as the result of adding water to strong cyder, or in the form of pirkin or ciderkin, the produce of re-worked pummice with added water. Such small cider would not only have helped to prevent the onset of scurvy, but to an extent would have replaced normal drinking water, which was often foul. Alternatively, strong cyder was taken on board to mix with the ship's water, making it more palatable. The Elizabethan surgeon William Clowes, discussing how the poor diet of sailors caused scurvy, said that their best drink was a "beveridge" of wine and the putrefied ship's water.[84] "Beverage" at the time regularly indicated either wine or cider, both re-worked and watered. The use of cyder in this way may well have been the result of a deliberate search for a healthy shipboard drink by the educated men of the Renaissance, who were as concerned with natural philosophy as with economic and political patriotism. Francis Bacon, who became Lord Verulam and (in 1618) James I's Lord Chancellor, advising George Villiers of the pleasure and profit of planting orchards, observed that "Cider and Perry are notable beverages in sea voyages". Paradoxically the special use of the term "beverage" is further evidence for the wine-strength cyder of the time. Bacon himself tells us that the contemporary cyderists (in 1605) took great pains to achieve full ripeness in the fruit: "For they take care not to bruise or squeeze the apples till they have lain together for a while in heaps, and so ripened by mutual contact."[85] Bacon believed this practice was in fact borrowed from the vineyard, where the grower turned round the bunches of grapes to face the sun to ensure a uniform ripening, and it was surely an essential step in the production of a full, rich liquor.

Bacon also reconstructs for his reader the desperation of early voyagers after six months at sea with the onset of scurvy: "So that finding our Selves, in the midst of the greatest Wildernesse of waters in the world, without Victual, we gave ourselves up for lost Men, and prepared for Death."[86] Yet scorbutic voyagers were snatched from death, Bacon knew, by timely draughts of cyder: in his *New Atlantis*, a vision of an ideal and scientific society, arriving travellers were greeted with cyder and oranges, "an assured remedy for sicknesse taken at sea". Those with special knowledge of horticulture also knew of the antiscorbutic properties of cyder, and Parkinson observes in his botanical and herbal work, ". . . yea many Hogsheads and Tunnes are made especially to be carried to the Sea in long voyages, and is found by experience to bee of excellent use, to mix with water for beverage".[87]

While cyder kept better on board ship than fresh fruit, it did not keep for ever, and as with use it descended in the barrel so would it be contaminated by the air and slowly turn acetous, losing also its antiscorbutic properties. This problem was felt very early, and attempts were made to overcome it. Very shortly after the return of James Lancaster's squadron, Sir Henry Platt[88] was busy selling a nostrum which he called "philosophical fire" which, he claimed, would preserve food and "beverage" in long voyages. "Beverage" includes "Wine, Perrie, Sider, Beere, Ale and Vinegar" and perhaps the habit of taking these drinks to sea goes back to Drake and Hawkins, whom Platt claims to have supplied with food (macaroni) on their last voyages. Platt's "philosophical fire" was in the form of a powder which he claimed had a "sympatheticall nature with all plants and Animals". In fact Platt's commodity seems to have been a species of "sympathetic powder" which caught a fashionable imagination of the time.

"Sympathy" was a virtue or force communicating between two distant objects (we shall see below that the cyder fruit tree was sympathetic to the peach and antipathetic to the walnut) and was essentially mysterious. It was in fact precisely the kind of "occult" power that the followers of Bacon and of the new science of the seventeenth century were opposed to, and it seems that it was to meet some such criticism that Platt called his powder "philosophical", that is, "scientific". Likewise, Sir Kenelm Digby, impressing the courts of Europe with a sympathetic powder that cured wounds at a distance (it was anhydrous copper sulphate, prepared with much astrological ceremony), was careful to explain its powers in terms of the newly modish atoms of the day.

In contrast to such ideas was the empirical knowledge of the antiscorbutic effect of cyder and fruit juice. This knowledge was possessed by some men in four main groups, the apothecaries and surgeons; the ships' officers and naval authorities; the physicians; and the cyderists, but it was not known to all men in these groups, nor was it readily communicated between the groups. Clowes and Platt knew of Lancaster's use of lemon juice during the East India voyage, but as a surgeon and apothecary, they wrote in English and were probably ignored by the physicians, who communicated in Latin. The ship's surgeon Woodall, writing specifically for surgeons in the service of the East India Company, also wrote in English: all three authors were ignored by the "discoverer" of the use of lemon juice in the eighteenth century, James Lind, whose survey of earlier literature on the subject is impressive, but restricted almost entirely to works in Latin. Of these four groups, it seems that it was the cyderists who kept alive the notion that cyder cured scurvy. Evelyn's correspondent[89] called cyder "specifically sovereign against the Scorbut", a sentiment repeated by Worlidge in 1676. We may imagine that one or more of the many editions of Evelyn's *Pomona* found its way into the libraries of eighteenth-century country gentlemen who had trees and fruit to look after, and it was as a cyderist and physician that the West Countryman John Huxham recommended, in 1747, that sailors should drink at least a pint of cider a day, the rougher the better, to keep scurvy at bay. He preferred its efficacy to that of oranges and lemons, and it may be that his experience was derived from the product of his own orchard as it was certainly gained from the scorbutic sailors coming ashore at Plymouth. Many ships fitted out at Plymouth carried cyder as a result of Huxham's advice.

Huxham's interest in scurvy was part of a wider picture. In the 1740s, after a long period of peace, England was at war and it was a war of a new kind. The War of Jenkin's Ear involved the harassment of Spanish ships in the Caribbean, and the subsequent War of the Austrian Succession soon saw the English blockading the French fleet in its ports for long periods. Naval power was now seen as the foundation of British success in a theatre of war that ranged over the Atlantic to Canada and the American colonies. The sailors of the ships of the line, and not only of the merchantmen, were now on board for long periods, and almost overnight scurvy became an important problem. Huxham's essay of 1747 was not published until 1750, and meanwhile a number of other medical men were gathering experience of the value of cyder. Edward Ives, surgeon on board the *Yarmouth* (70 guns) with Admiral Martin, about 1740, had lost the usual high number of men to scurvy, when the idea occurred to him that cyder might serve as well as other vegetable juices (which seem not to have been available), and on finding that his admiral had heard the suggestion elsewhere, several hogsheads of the best South Hams cyder were taken on board as soon as possible, with good results: Ives prescribed a quart per patient per day, and lost no one (of a complement of 500) while the cyder lasted. The men who took the cyder were treated in precisely the same way as those when the cyder had gone, so the contrast was marked. Ives kept a journal from 1743 while he was on board the *Kent* in the East Indies, where he had success with lemon juice and rum. This use of cyder was known to Lind both from the journal and by letter before his own famous experiments of 1747. James Lind was surgeon of the *Salisbury*, a ship of comparable size to Ives's *Yarmouth*, and drawing upon the earlier experience of Ives and others, he performed a clinical trial upon twelve of his scurvy cases. To two of his patients he gave fresh oranges and lemons, to two more a daily quart of cyder and to the rest popular antiscorbutic receipts of the time. By the time the *Salisbury* sailed into Plymouth a month later the sailors who had taken the fresh fruit were cured; the treatment of the others continued only for two weeks, but even then those who had taken the cyder were clearly improving, despite the fact that the cyder was "indeed not very sound, being inclinable to be aigre or pricked".[90] However, the remaining patients had not improved at all.

Notwithstanding the fact that scurvy was a naval problem, it seems probable that Ives and Lind drew from a cyderists', not a sailors', tradition that cyder is good for scurvy. The same can be said of Huxham. His essay was not published until 1750, and Lind's results not until 1753, and it seems likely that the references in the cyder literature of the 1750s were likewise derived from cyderists' tradition rather than from medical publications: thus Ellis's *Compleat Cyderman* of 1754 claims that cyder is the antidote to gout and scurvy, "our reigning *British Disease*". Likewise Stafford's *Dissertation* of 1759 gives special attention to the cyder from crab apples as a "sovereign *antiscorbutic*". The work of Thomas Hale that was gathered together and published in 1756 as *A Compleat Body of Husbandry* also speaks of the antiscorbutic virtues of cyder.

Despite the knowledge of the cyderists, despite clear clinical trials of Ives and Lind and despite almost two centuries of knowledge of the usefulness of lemon juice among medical and nautical men, it was not until nearly the end of the eighteenth century that lime juice was issued to sailors as a matter of course, and then it was the work of an administrator, Sir Gilbert Blane, and not a doctor or an admiral. Cyder leaves the story with Lind, and we can only afford space here to correct one mistake still made by historians and dieticians about cyder and scurvy.

The mode of action of cyder and fruit juice upon scorbutic patients was, as we saw, quite unknown, and the result of its action was purely empirical knowledge. At an early date it was thought that scurvy was not contagious or infectious, because whatever the state of the crew, the officers rarely contracted the disease. This, in view of the officers' superior diet, was entirely explicable in terms of fundamental notions of dietetic causes of disease. It was then clear that the treatment and prevention of scurvy was a question of finding a complete diet, but the notion of a "deficiency disease" was not born until 1907 and as late as

1920 the idea was still alive that scurvy could be infective, because it was seen in laboratory animals with theoretically com plete diets.[91] Only with the recognition of vitamins was it seen that it was only the vitamin C in fruit juice that was necessary for the prevention of scurvy. Vitamin C is present in a number of fresh foods, particularly fruit and vegetables, but is rapidly oxidized, particularly in alkaline solution, and is destroyed in most means of preserving foods. Even lemon juice loses 80 per cent of its vitamin C in half an hour on exposure to air in an alkaline solution. Salt pork, dried beef, ships' biscuit and "portable soup", the diet of the common sailor, would have contained no vitamin C whatever, and scurvy was inevitable.

How effective would cyder have been in curing scurvy? Modern figures in common use give to us the surprising answer that it would *not* have been effective, for figures of the vitamin C content of various foods and drinks, widely accepted in the medical world, suggest that cider contains *no* vitamin C,[92] or at the best "a trace".[93] This has led to a reappraisal of Lind's experiments and his scientific method: how could his patients have improved with cyder, if it contained no vitamin C?[94]

The answer brings us face to face once more with the difference between, and the history of, cyder and cider. "The best South Hams cyder" that Ives used in his experiment was of wine strength, the result of no other process than natural fermentation; the cider of the modern food-tables is dilute, and the samples used may well have been pasteurized to stop fermentation in the bottle, a process which would help to destroy the vitamin C. Figures for vitamin C content are "traditional" within the medical literature, being often quoted but infrequently tested. In re-examining Lind's experiments a recent author[95] has very properly reassessed the vitamin C content of cider and found that it contains 3.3 milligrams per litre, which is indeed "a trace". But cyder, *made in the way it was made in the eighteenth century*, contains ten times as much. Figures vary somewhat with the variety of fruit, but a popular bittersweet like Strawberry Norman in the season 1978–9 produced a cyder with 33.8 milligrams per litre. The variation among commercial ciders is great, and while the average figure is well below that of real cyder, Bulmer's Strongbow gave a figure approaching that of cyder;

and the laurels must be awarded to the fine produce of an old family of cyderists, Symonds' Scrumpy Jack, which gave a figure of 47 milligrams per litre.[96]

Medical Research Council experiments in 1948 showed that as little as 5 milligrams per day – about a wine glass full of Scrumpy Jack – will prevent scurvy. Two wine glasses will begin to relieve the symptoms[97] but a severely scorbutic man could absorb several hundred times this amount of the vitamin. A healthy man cannot absorb more than is contained in about two or three pints of real cyder – the dose given by Ives and Lind – and this would have been plenty to make the most desperately ill sailor recover.

Recovery was dramatic. The severely scorbutic sailor was *in extremis*: his teeth had become so loose that they were in danger of falling out; his gums were swollen with spongy flesh so that eating was difficult, and his breath was so foul that even a hardened ship's surgeon could hardly bear to come close. His inelastic flesh retained the impressions made by the fingers of the surgeon who examined him; his legs were covered with purplish-black ulcers; old scars dissolved and became wounds again and fractures healed perhaps twenty years before once more opened up. An effort to rise from his bed, or even the experience of being carried from his quarters into the fresh air could mean sudden death. In the last stages of the disease the sailor was wont to faint away at the least exertion, and was plagued by dangerous haemorrhages. Imagine, then, the change that occurs, even at this stage, when the first hogshead of South Hams cyder, newly brought on board, is tapped and the surgeon brings the first pint to the dying sailor: he struggles to raise his head, and with help he drinks it. The effort almost overcomes him, but at once the acid works its subtle chemistry in his starved tissues, and at once he feels better; after the second, and perhaps third, pint of his daily dose some hope stirs within his mind. After forty-eight hours the signs of recovery are clear to the surgeons, and after a week the sailor is on his feet and will shortly resume his duties.

The cyder used in treating scurvy was made in Devon, being readily available to the ports on the south coast. It differed in many ways from the Herefordshire cyder, both in the manner of making it and in its effects on the body.

Early in the eighteenth century the medical writer William Musgrave, writing on arthritis, recorded a particular kind of colic that appeared in Devon in those seasons when a great deal of cyder was drunk (perhaps at harvest). It appeared most severely in those who drank the most, and Musgrave had no hesitation in attributing the "Devonshire colic" to the "rough and acid cider". Huxham also noticed the seasonal variation in the disease, and gave a graphic account of the symptoms, including the "excessively tormenting pain in the stomach", the "unequal weak pulse, and coldish sweats", and the "enormous vomiting . . . of exceeding green bile".[98] Huxham also thought that the colic was caused by the rawness and roughness of the cyder. The dangers of cyder from his own part of Devon, the South Hams, had been remarked on at least as early as 1753.[99]

But in the 1760s it began to appear that there was something unusual about the cyder-colic of Devon. The first thing was that it did not appear in the counties of Hereford, Gloucester and Worcester. It was natural, then, to compare the two kinds of cyder in an attempt to find the cause of the colic: George Baker, who like Huxham came from the South Hams, probably Devon's most well-known cyder-producing area, found that the poorer people of Herefordshire and the neighbouring counties "use, as their common drink, a weak acid cyder". It was not, then, the *acidity* of the cyder, and Baker had other evidence that acidity as such had little deleterious effect. It seemed to Baker that the symptoms of Devon colic, often terminating in paralysis of the limbs and even death, were identical to those of lead poisoning. This condition was known at the time in those concerned with the mining and manufacture of lead; moreover, the effects of lead in wine were known, arising either from accidental contamination or, more often, from deliberate use of lead compounds to correct the sourness of the wine. This practice was known to the Romans, but its harmful effects were not known. Adulteration of wine in this way continued through the Middle Ages, but by Baker's time the harm resulting from the practice was well known, and chemists were now able to identify lead in adulterated wine. Baker took advantage of this and, taking some Devon cyder back with him to London, where he now lived, found considerable quantities of lead in it. He was able to show that these soluble lead compounds entered the cyder during its manufacture, for it was common in Devon to seal the joints between the stones which composed the trough of the mill with metallic lead. Often enough, it appears, the stones did not fit very well, perhaps because of the difficulty of hewing the native granite (Herefordshire cyder mills are made of the more easily worked sandstone) and the lead-filled gaps were often large. Moreover, it was not uncommon for the bases of the wooden presses to be lined with sheet lead to prevent leakage. Sometimes lead pipes were used to direct the cyder from the presses, and sometimes lead shot was placed in the vessels to prevent the cyder turning sour.

Baker was now in a slightly awkward position. He was obliged, as a doctor, to publish his results (he did so in 1767, after the paper had been read to the College of Physicians in London) but at the same time he appeared to be attacking his fellow Devonians either for their honest ignorance that metallic lead would contaminate the cyder, or, by implication, for their deliberate adulteration of the finished product. Cyder was one of the principal exports of Devon,[100] and its producers were naturally alarmed that it should get a bad reputation. Many sprang to the defence of the product, but in the face of Baker's evidence, and the admission lists of the hospitals at harvest time, the best they could do was to insist that, yes, there was colic, but it was due to the acidity of the cyder, and not lead poisoning. In the pamphlet war that followed it came out that the farmers of Dorset, at least, were in the habit of buying sugar of lead from the apothecaries for the purpose of sweetening cyder. Another source of the lead was pointed out some years later by James Hardy, who discovered that the cyder was often stored in earthenware vessels with a lead-containing glaze.

The whole unfortunate episode in the history of cyder provides us with a clue as to the fate of wine-strength cyder. From the remark of George Baker, quoted above, and from a pamphlet published by Francis Geach, surgeon to the Plymouth hospital (arguing that acidity alone was the cause of colic), it is clear that the poorer inhabitants of Herefordshire and its neighbouring counties drank "weak" cider. Baker and Geach, as Devonians, must have been struck by the water added to the apple juice during the making of cider in Herefordshire. In the South Hams water cider was that made from fallings[101] and "beverage" was the weak but unwatered last pressing, which could only be preserved by the addition of spices.[102] Both these forms of weak cider were very distinct from the bulk of the produce. We have already examined a number of reasons for the practice of watering the cider in Herefordshire and we are left to conclude that undiluted, wine-strength cyder, still drunk by the upper classes in Herefordshire, was much more common among all classes in Devon. Indeed, some effort seems to have been put into making their cyder as strong as possible: we shall look briefly at the evidence for this a little below, and here we must conclude that the lead poisoning episode must be one of the reasons why the tradition of strong cyder has not survived down to the twentieth century. Perhaps the trade in Devon cyder did decline when the purchasing public in the big towns (we hear of London and Westminster) heard the rumours of lead poisoning. Certainly nineteenth-century medical reports indicate that cases became less as the century wore on:[103] no doubt some of the lead was taken from the mills and presses, and in any case the old horse-mill was gradually replaced by mobile machinery of wood and iron. Perhaps Herefordshire methods of production were copied, or perhaps payment of wages in cider became more common; and there is no doubt that Devon shared the conditions suffered by the rest of the country which were unrewarding for the continuation of the cyder habit.

So anxious were the cyderists of Devon to produce strong cyder that it was not an uncommon practice to boil the freshly pressed juice until its volume was reduced by about half. The effect of this was undoubtedly to drive off the water that is naturally present in the juice, and so to concentrate the remaining sugar and other heavy molecules that give the cyder its taste. There is some evidence that the boiling was supposed to reduce the "windy" quality of cyder,[104] which we met in the writing of Andrew Boorde in the sixteenth century, but it seems more likely that it was an attempt to prevent the cyder from becoming too sharp. It is a common fault of fully fermented cyder that the conversion of the sugar into alcohol leaves manifest the taste of

the fruit acids, and most modern ciders are secondarily and artificially sweetened. Most likely the great concentration of sugar in
eighteenth-century boiled cyder was not totally consumed in fermentation and left a residual sweetness to blend with the sharp
and astringent components of the juice.

John Newburgh, a contributor to Evelyn's *Pomona*, reports of
the practice in the seventeenth century that boiled cyder would
keep for two years, while that left untreated kept a year only. It
was sometimes said that Devon cyder did not keep so well as
that of Herefordshire, but it was during this period that the practice of bottling the racked cyder began (so giving a life perhaps
ten times as long) and it is not always clear from the accounts
which method is being used. But no one in Herefordshire boiled
their cyder. Captain Sylas Taylor, another contributor to
Evelyn's *Pomona*, argued against it from a Hereford standpoint in
the seventeenth century, and Philips in the eighteenth claimed
that the cyders of his native soil needed no such stratagems to
improve them:

> . . . nor let the crude humours dance
> In heated brass, steaming with fire intense;
> Altho' *Devonia* much commends the use
> Of strengthening *Vulcan*; with their native strength
> Thy wines sufficient, other aid refuse;
> And, when th'allotted orb of time's compleat,
> Are more commended than the labour'd drinks.

It is not clear what kind of vessel the cyder was boiled in, but
those made of metal would have obvious advantages, like
Philips's "heated brass", as well as obvious dangers, if an alloy
containing lead was used. It seems also to have been at this stage
that the glazed earthenware vessels were used that were claimed
by Hardy to be a cause of lead poisoning. Indeed several of the
experiments performed by Baker and Hardy seem to suggest
that the cyder was actually boiled in glazed vessels.

Part Two

An idealized view of a cyder orchard, from the 1776 edition of
Philips's poem "Cyder". The artist has drawn planting, grafting and
ripe fruit together in the same season. The small mill in the background is shown without harness

Introduction

In the first part of this book we discussed the history and disappearance of cyder. This section is a plea for the revival of cyder and a description of how it should be made. In arguing for this revival the historical evidence for the old techniques is presented as a guide to modern practice; the topics are treated in the sequence of the cyderist's year, from planting the tree to tapping the barrel.

With the introduction of modern orcharding techniques and a growth in demand for cider, it is once again possible for the prospective ciderist to buy a piece of land and plant a new orchard with the purpose of selling the fruit and seeing economic return from his investment. Previously, old orchards were kept going by the piecemeal replacement of old trees, which was easier and cheaper than returning the soil to some other form of husbandry; but in creating a *new* orchard the ciderist is in the position of his seventeenth-century predecessor when English cyder was at its height.

The cost of hauling the fruit to the factories of the big firms in practice limits the area in which large-scale orchards can be economically established, but it is still very worth while for anyone who lives where apples can grow to devote part of his land or garden, or to buy a plot, for the purpose of making his own cyder in the traditional (but not modern) way for the consumption of himself, his family and his friends. He will have the satisfaction of reviving a centuries-old practice and producing a natural, wine-strength drink, without additives and without the aid of a pre-packaged kit, of superb delicacy and flavour.

Location

Let us imagine ourselves in the ideal position of a cyderist whose sole aim is to make the most excellent possible cyder, and who has at his disposal the means of doing so. In seeing what such a man would do, and in fact *did* do, historically, we can learn many things that will be of use in our actual, less-than-ideal, situations.

He would first look round for a suitable location for his orchard. He would be free to choose anywhere in the Midlands and south of England, avoiding the north as too cold for the late-maturing fruit. We have seen that the modern preponderance of growing cider-fruit in the West came about simply because it was more profitable in the South-east to grow and sell table-fruit direct to London, leaving the distant West Country to produce a durable product that would survive transportation. The east of England is sunnier than the west, which can only be beneficial for the slow-ripening cider apple, but the experienced cyderist would be very careful to choose a spot not over-exposed to the cold east winds of spring in East Anglia. The greater rainfall of the west would allow him to take a crop of hay, or graze sheep below standard, or half-standard trees, but for the moment we will assume that his orchard will be the more prolific bush trees. Apart from the mainland, the Channel Islands have long featured in the history of cyder, no doubt both because of their warm climate and because they lay between France and England when the cyder habit spread across the Channel. With the enclosure of waste ground, the moderately well-to-do planted orchards contained within high banks, and by Tudor times cyder making was a minor industry. In the time of Charles II cyder was a staple drink and 24,000 hogsheads were produced annually in Jersey alone, much of it for export.[1]

With very little geographical restriction on the location of an orchard, the next question is one of topographical location. The ideal site is a south-facing slope, and it is very important that the site be protected from the north-east. The planter in previous centuries believed that the wind from the opposite quarter, the south-west, or west, personalized by the Romans as Favonius or Zephyrus, the warm wet wind that blew at the beginning of spring, actually had powers of generation all its own. Virgil's

Ore omnes versae in Zephyros stant rupibus altis,
Exceptantque leves auras[2]

was translated by Dryden as

The mares to Cliffs of rugged Rock repair,
And with wide Nostrils snuff the Western Air . . .

continuing

When (wondrous to relate) the Parent Wind,
Without the Stallion, propagates the Kind.

The "cyder poet", John Philips, expressed the idea thus in the early eighteenth century:

Who'er expects his lab'ring trees shou'd bend
With fruitage, and a kindly harvest yield,
Be this his first concern, to find a tract
Impervious to the winds, begirt with hills
That intercept the *Hyperborean* blasts
Tempestuous, and cold Eurus' nipping force,
Noxious to feeble buds: but to the west
Let him free entrance grant, let Zephyrs bland
Administer their tepid genial airs;
Nought fear he from the west, whose gentle warmth
Discloses well the earth's all-teeming womb . . .

The "earth's all-teeming womb" is not merely an expression referring to the fertility of the earth, but it represents a pre-scientific-revolution idea that the whole world and all its parts is *alive* and growing, with a universal life-force or world soul, a notion Philips shared with Worlidge. The life force was not equally present in all places, and was reflected in the kind of vegetation. All plants, possessing a share of the common force of life, were thought to be in some way aware of each other's existence, and able to react to it. There were, that is, sympathies and antipathies between plants, and also between animals and minerals, each having its share of life (compare the phrase the "living rock"). Philips tells us that the cyder tree is sympathetic to peach, hazel, palm, quince and elder, but because of its antipathy, it should not be planted close to walnut or cherry.

Soil

Poetic licence enabled Philips to use such non-scientific ideas which were out of date even to the scientists of the seventeenth century, and Evelyn and his friends in the Royal Society would have been sceptical of such sympathies. In seeking to produce the best cyder, they were concerned to collect systematically empirical evidence as to the siting of an orchard and, the topic that would be the next concern of our prospective cyderist, the nature of the soil. "He that would treat exactly of *Cider* and *Perry*, must lay his Foundation so deep as to begin with the *Soil*," says Dr Beale in opening his "General Advertisements concerning Cider". The general theory underlying seventeenth-century descriptions of the soil and its produce was the notion, sometimes half-forgotten in a rapidly changing age, that the natural world was characterized, indeed in a sense composed, of four elementary Qualities, Hot, Dry, Cold and Wet which we met above. Those of the body reacted directly with those of the world at large, particularly the body's immediate environment. For example in the absence of a germ theory of disease, the ancient and renaissance physician considered that disease was partly due to the nature of the winds of the locality, including the Favonius we have already met, and the Qualitative nature of the soil over which the winds had passed.

Like the human body, fruit trees were thought to react favourably to soils that suited their Qualitative composition. There was widespread agreement in the seventeenth century that cyder trees liked Hot soils, particularly that which had previously borne rye.[3] The soil of Herefordshire has a deep-red colour derived from the underlying Old Red Sandstone, with the exception of a pear-shaped outcrop of the older Silurian shale centred on the village of Woolhope, the Woolhope Dome. The contrast is marked, and the slippery shale agrees well with the old theory in appearing Cold and Wet to the senses. The Qualities of the soil were thought to be transferred, at least to begin with, into the cyder: the "hot and sandy" soil of King's Capel and the rich red clay and sand of Holme Lacy were thought to be particularly suitable for the most celebrated of all cyder fruit, the Herefordshire Redstreak, and in these two villages it was said to produce perhaps the finest cyder in the county.[4] The cyder of the Woolhope Dome was generally wheyish in colour, like the soil, but the skill of the inhabitants was such that it was often brought to near perfection as a lighter cyder.[5]

So warm and light soils were invariably favoured for cyder fruit, and most of our sources advise against "cold and wet" clays and heavy soils. It was not regarded as essential to plant new trees in rich soil, and Philips reproved those farmers who with "fatning muck/Besmear the roots". It was generally agreed that perry pear trees grew admirably in soils too thin and gravelly for cyder fruit.

Few modern cyderists will be in a position to achieve these old ideals as to soil, and must be content with what they have. But we should not despair, for cyder fruit trees are not choosy about the nature of the soil, nor does the quality of the soil affect the quality of the cyder, at least in the way they thought in the seventeenth and eighteenth centuries. One important rule is to avoid damp patches. Apple trees "like to keep their feet dry" and it may be, as Philips warns us, that miry fields produce beautiful apples but poor cyder.

Philips also advises against chalky soil, "stubborn and jejune":

The Must, of pallid hue, declares the soil
Devoid of spirit; wretched he that quaffs
Such wheyish liquors, oft with cholic pangs
With pungent cholic pangs distress'd he'll roar
And toss and turn and curse th' unwholesome draught.

But the modern cyderist should not be dismayed if his soil is
chalky; it is unlikely that Philips's account is more than a poetic
transfer of the qualities of the soil to the cyder, and in any case
the alkalinity of the soil can be redressed by the addition of
compost, dung, or the pummice that remains after the must has
been pressed from it.

Varieties

What, then, should our cyderist plant, having considered the
matter of site and soil? Here the historical evidence can help him
only in a limited way: we know the *kind* of apples that make good
cyder, but we cannot reproduce the great cyders of the seventeenth and eighteenth centuries because the actual varieties have
since perished. We can only read and wonder about the great
Redstreak that was the foundation of the fame of Herefordshire
cyder, for we cannot now taste it. We can only guess at the
flavour of the cyder that Charles I preferred to wine during his
unhappy sojourn in Hereford.
The reason for this is that there is no such thing as a self-

perpetuating variety of fruit tree: each variety of apple is genetically a single *individual*: each variety is a unique genetic
combination which determines the balance of organic compounds that gives the fruit its taste but which is lost at every fertilization. While the fruit faithfully reproduces the characteristics
of the tree, as soon as its seeds (which contain genes from *another*
individual) germinate, then the new individual is genetically different and its fruit quite different in taste.

The discovery of a fruit good for cyder is then a matter of
chance and once discovered, the tree must be propagated by veg-
etative means, in which there is no genetical disturbance. The
means of doing this is by grafting, in which a piece of the original
tree is physically inserted into the body of another and allowed
to bear fruit. Although physically separated in this way, and
however many times the fragments of the original tree are
grafted and regrafted to produce thousands of trees, genetically
they remain one individual, and like an individual the variety
grows old, becomes more liable to canker and other diseases,
finally becoming sterile and uneconomic to propagate.

The historical evidence suggests that a variety of apple suitable
for making cyder would last perhaps a century and a half (perry
pear varieties were longer lived,[6] the individual trees often
reaching great age and size). It was necessary to experiment and
search out new varieties by crossing favoured existing varieties
and keeping an eye open for the fortuitous crab that could be cultivated. This search for new varieties is the reason for the flood of
different named varieties that overwhelm the historian. Apart
from the Redstreak, the famous cyder apples of the seventeenth
and eighteenth centuries were the Gennet-Moyle, Foxwhelp,
Styre apple, Hagloe crab, Leather coat, Oaken pin, Gillyflower,
and Whitesour. Many names indicate a French origin, like the
Deux-ans; indeed in the nineteenth century there were reckoned
to be some five hundred different kinds of cyder apple in
France.[7]

It is possible that the genetic shake-up at each fertilization of
popular varieties, although not perpetuating the varieties,
nevertheless produced among their offspring natural *groups* of
fruit, some having the sweetness of the known parent, another
its astringency, some no doubt as inedible as crabs, and some-

having characteristics of the unknown parent. Of course, cross-fertilization between *similar* trees is more likely in a large orchard, or fruit-growing area, and this would increase the chances of attractive natural groupings within the mixed offspring. William of Malmesbury, writing in the thirteenth century of the cider-producing county Gloucestershire, describes such ungrafted natural varieties: "Cernas tramites publicos vestitos pomiferis arboribus, non insitiva manus industria, sed ipsius solius humi natura",[8] that is, "You may see the public pathways lined with apple trees, not grafted by the skill of the hand but [arising] from the nature of the soil itself alone". *Non insitiva* is "not grafted": the technique of grafting was known to the Romans, and the emphasis here is on the suitability of the soil.

Possibly some of the old varieties of the Middle Ages were such natural groups or "varieties". The Warden pear, used in making perry, appears on the arms of the Cistercian monks of Warden in Bedfordshire. "Pearmain" and "costard" are two names of thirteenth-century varieties of apples that apparently survived longer than we should expect: either they were naturally recurring types or the names were shifted to related grafted varieties.

So, as observed at the beginning of this section, we know from historical evidence the *kinds* of varieties of apple to plant to make good cyder, even though we cannot know the taste of the old varieties. Cyder fruit has a balance of three major elements – sugar, tannin and acid – that is different from table or "pot" fruit. The sugar produces the alcohol, the tannin gives the cyder a bite – the "generous roughness" of the seventeenth century – and the acid prevents the cyder from having a flat taste. Cyder fruit has *less* acid than table fruit because in the finished cyder the acid is no longer masked by the sugar and is much more obvious. Also, the tannin content of cyder fruit is higher, so that in general the fruit is uneatable from the tree. The same is true of perry pears, and the famous Barland pear of the eighteenth century was said to be inedible even for pigs.

Within this broad description of cyder fruit there have been, since the great days of cyder making in the seventeenth century, recognized categories in which the balance of the main elements is different. "Bittersweets" are those with a balance such that no other apples need to be added to make cyder; but the basic staple component can be varied to achieve different effects by the addition of "sweets", which are low in tannin and acid, and of "sharps", which are high in acid.

The bittersweets in particular are late-ripening varieties, perhaps reflecting their origin in warmer countries. They are also late flowering, an important characteristic to be borne in mind when planting in a spot given to frost. A modern supplier of young trees, like Bulmer's, have both medium and late varieties of bittersweets, and are happy to give advice on planting. Historically bittersweets were known as "winter fruit" which were not ground and pressed until November or December and the strong juice of which – real cyder – lasted throughout the year. In contrast summer cider was made early in the season from a variety of apples, most often with a great deal of water; it had to be drunk quickly as it would not outlast the cold weather. In the earlier period "hard" cider was distinguished from "soft" on the same grounds, and reflected the presence of the principle of bitterness, tannin.

The modern cyderist then, should plant almost entirely recognized varieties of bittersweet. Yarlington Mill, Dabinett and Ball's Bitter Sweet are admirable varieties giving a balanced cyder. If a little more acidity is required Tom Putt is a useful addition, although it is an old variety and may not be readily available. Another old variety of excellence is White Beech, which has so much tannin that the raw, newly fermented juice is almost undrinkable, like some clarets, but a few months in an oak cask produces a distinguished cyder. Brown Snout is a modern variety that is also high in tannin and worth growing.

While the taste of the old varieties is gone, there are enough descriptions by contemporaries for us to see what the experts of the time were looking for, characteristics which are still a valuable guide today. This applies in particular to the Redstreak, which prompted an encomium from the lips of all who tasted it. This apple owes its existence to Lord Scudamore, Charles I's ambassador to France. There, it is said, he became interested in French fruit and cyder, and, on returning to his native Herefordshire, he had the good fortune to raise the Redstreak from a planted seed, as a "wilding" or "crab". For many years, indeed, it was known as "Scudamore's crab", and was quickly and widely propagated by grafting. Evelyn gratefully recalls that it was by "*the noble Example of my Lord* Scudamore, *and of some other public-spirited* Gentlemen *in those parts* [that] *all* Herefordshire *is become, in a manner, but one intire* Orchard".

The Redstreak is said to have been a "hard" apple, that is, astringent (to the point of being inedible) and late-ripening. Both features accounted for its "generous roughness" and its keeping qualities.[9] Evelyn retells the story of the London wine-merchant we have already met, who, visiting Herefordshire, was wagered he could not produce a French or Spanish wine better than Redstreak cyder. Twice he tried, before independent judges, and twice he failed.[10] The Redstreak was the pre-eminent fruit for Beale, who spoke of its "mordicant Sweetness [which] most agreeably gives the Farewel, endearing the relish to all fragrant *Palats*".[11] We also know that Redstreak cyder was of a reddish-yellow colour, derived from the purple colour of the fruit, and possessing a highly aromatic "nose": "The *Taste*, like the *Flavour*, or *Perfume* of excellent *Peaches*, very grateful to the *Palate* and *Stomach*", as Captain Sylas Taylor observed.[12] The cyder was of full body and "oily", and on "drawing a cork out of a bottle of this cyder, you are regaled with a most delightful odour, such as proceeds from no other"; a flavour which was compared to dried angelica roots in the list of cyder fruit that accompanies Stafford's *Treatise* of 1759. By this time the decline of the Redstreak's vigour was obvious. Before his own death in 1708, the cyder poet left us tantalizing imagery of the Redstreak at its height, draining his glass of the very cyder as he wrote:

> See! the numbers flow
> Easy, whilst, chear'd with her nectareous juice,
> Hers, and my country's praises I exalt.
> Hail *Herefordian* plant, that dost disdain
> All other fields! Heav'n's sweetest blessing, hail!

Planting

The one thing that determines how cyder trees should be planted is what is grown underneath them. Undoubtedly the highest return, in a commercial sense, is from bush trees planted close together with no undercrop. But it is also possible to combine two different kinds of husbandry and plant half-standard trees further apart, allowing sheep to graze below the trees. The extra rainfall of the west makes this a frequent combination, but there may be parts of eastern England where the lower rainfall and lighter soils would make this impossible. It is also possible to plant standard trees at even greater distances to allow cattle to graze below.

These different combinations were worked out in the days when cyder was in its prime, and when other techniques were also used. Cyder trees were not only planted on land previously used for rye (because of the superior nature of the soil), but they were also planted on land that continued to be planted with rye. When the enclosure was large, anything between twenty and one hundred acres, standard trees would be planted some fifty or sixty feet apart to allow for the passage of the plough between them and below the branches. Perhaps this was simply an extension of the practice of planting the trees in the hedges, to that of planting in the field itself, as cyder fruit increasingly proved to be a valuable crop. Likewise trees were planted in grazing land, and Beale, in Evelyn's *Pomona*, describes a technique of planting trees, each on a mound surrounded by prickly bushes and a circular ditch, that protected the trees from cattle.

The specialist cyder orchard perhaps only came in with the Redstreak which, as a "dwarf" tree, could only be protected from livestock by enclosing the entire orchard in a stock-proof fence. Because there was no undercrop, it was planted close, about sixteen feet separating the trees. The modern cyderist will also do best with such a purpose-built orchard if he is thinking in terms of quantity, but it is still good advice after more than three and a half centuries to plant cyder trees in hedgerows; and in modern farms, in odd corners out of reach of mechanization.

Grafting

The modern cyderist will buy his trees already grafted, and so has no need to concern himself with grafting. He must, however accept what he is sold by the supplier, and although these will normally be the proper bittersweets and other kinds of cyder fruit, there can be minor disadvantages. First, modern cyder fruit is bred for its size. Many old varieties of tree produce very small fruit, which makes bending down to fill a bag with them hard work. Larger apples are more efficiently handled, and so are favoured by the grower who sells them to a big cider manufacturer. The manufacturer in turn has the resources to produce a balanced cider out of a mixture of fruit irrespective of whether or not the modern fruit has lost some of the quality of the old varieties in being selected for size.

The farmer of a century or more ago was less concerned with commercial efficiency than with the quality of the apple, upon which, without the resources of a modern manufacturer, he relied directly. He was quite prepared then to cultivate small fruit with a good reputation, and the extra effort involved in bagging the fruit was of no consequence at a time of year when he had spare labour.

Moreover, many of the old varieties were selected for their excellence in producing strong cyder, while modern varieties are bred for characteristics, not necessarily the same, which are useful in making modern cider a long drink. Many of the old varieties still exist in old orchards or forgotten corners. In some cases their name has been forgotten as the property changed hands; in a few cases they are remembered and valued as old varieties without modern counterparts. It is still possible, then, for a cyderist to use apples that were meant for real cyder, from trees that were preserved because of their excellence. Most of these old trees, to be sure, are poor bearers and subject to disease, but the cyderist with a taste for cyder and for history, and who is not primarily interested in the financial efficiency of his orchard, can give the old varieties temporary new life by grafting. The famous Redstreak, alas, is gone for ever, but there are other varieties still surviving from the early nineteenth century to be tried. Some produce cyder with a rare aromatic "nose" or great body that is not found in modern varieties: it is only by experience that the cyderist will find that real cyder, made in the proper way, is so different a *kind* of drink that it might be thought to be not related at all to modern commercial ciders.

Another reason for the modern cyderist to take an interest in grafting is that he might find that some of the trees in his orchard bear more prolifically than others or produce cyder more suited to his palate. It is then good sense to graft scions of the favoured variety upon stocks of the other trees.

Grafting has been known at least since Roman times, and has generally excited wonder as a thing outside the course of nature: causing one tree to grow upon another. In ignorance of the causes of the phenomenon, all attention was given to the techniques that ensured success, and these were passed on from one generation to the next amid some superstition. Seventeenth-century writers like John Evelyn quote the Roman author Varro with great respect when discussing the manner of grafting, and seventeenth-century science was only beginning to throw off superstitions transmitted down the ages as folklore. It is on a basis of collective experience that Evelyn tells us that the crab-apple tree makes the best stock for grafting, on account of its vigour; but he is bending before the force of an ancient but seemingly rational idea when he says that the nature of the grafted fruit will be a mixture of the parent of the scion and the stock. This idea was widespread in Herefordshire, where they preferred to graft upon a Gennet-Moyle stock, already a very popular cyder variety, believing that its qualities would be mixed with those of the graft. We have already seen that it is the genetic make-up of the tree that determines the nature of the fruit, not the qualities of the nutriment supplied to it by the stock or the soil.

Contemporary with Evelyn were the naturalists Nehemiah Grew and the Italian Malpighi, who were making detailed studies of the structure of plants. It was on a basis of their work that grafting came to be better understood. The growth of trees was now seen to depend upon a very thin layer of cells between the outer bark and the inner wood. It then became clear that in grafting, this growing layer of the stock, the cambium, must at some point touch that of the scion to ensure the proper disposition of subsequent structural and conducting vessels.

Of the two most well-known methods of grafting, the whip method and crown grafting, the latter is to be preferred. In whip grafting the stock and scion are about the same diameter, which means that their layers of cambium, circles in cross-section, at best intersect and sometimes never meet, like concentric circles. In crown grafting, choose a limb of the stock tree greater than one inch in diameter and cut it off. Slit the bark of the stump as many times as there are scions (up to about half a dozen) and peel back, exposing the internal wood. The soft growing cambium is the layer that splits, so peeling back the bark reveals a broad expanse of cambium, and it is consequently easier to set the cambium of the scion against it. The cambium of the stock may be on the outside surface of the exposed wood or possibly on the inside surface of the peeled bark, so cut the scion on *both* sides, making a wedge, and push gently between the bark and wood. Bind up the graft with raffia or the kind of string that will rot away in a year or so (*not* nylon, which will remain and

86

strangle growth) and cover with grafting wax to keep the natural moisture in and the rain out.

Grafting should be carried out in April, when the sap is stirring but before the buds have broken. Many authors recommend that the scions should be cut several months earlier and kept in soil in a cool spot so that they are less advanced in the spring than the stock.

Gathering the fruit

The origin of the process and the kind of cyder it was designed to make stand revealed at two points during the making of real cyder. At these two points in the process the cyderist was trying to increase the sweetness of the finished product, firstly in

Matured apples on their way to be pressed

increasing the sugar content of the fruit and secondly by preventing excessive fermentation of the juice. The commonest fault of cyder and cider is that they can be too dry at the end of fermentation. Commercial cider-makers often pasteurize the result and replace the lost sweetness and sparkle artificially, but the amateur cyderist may not wish to do this, even if the equipment is available to him; nor may he wish to drink his cyder while it is still a little sweet but before the fermentation has finally clarified it, for then he will lose the chance of producing a fine mature cyder in bottle. The modern cyderist cannot do better than to follow the práctice of his seventeenth-century forebears.

We have seen that the best cyder fruit has always been that which ripened late. Indeed, it might be said that it ripens too late, and it was never good practice to use the fruit straight from the tree. No doubt this is a reflection of the southern origin of the cyder habit, where the warmer summers allowed an earlier pollination of the flowers and a longer autumn for the ripening of the fruit. The winter fruit of English cyder at its height fell from the tree before it was fully ripe, said the cyderists at the time. In

November those that had not fallen were shaken down, collected together, and placed in heaps out of the rain and away from the frost. Worlidge tells us that the fruit is ripe when the pips are black, but still the fruit should hang on the tree as long as possible afterwards.[13] How long to allow the apples to stand in heaps before milling was a disputed question. As the process was beneficial, the longer the better it seemed; yet there was the practical consideration that fruit a little over-ripe turned rather slimy in the mill and was difficult to press. Modern experience shows that such pulp blocks the pores of the hair cloth in the press and prevents the easy escape of juice: increased pressure causes the unseparated pulp to leap from the pores in the cloth like so much toothpaste pressed from the tube.

It was generally agreed however that winter ("hard") fruit should stand longer than other sorts, and the Redstreak was often not milled and pressed before January, having stood some six weeks, as recommended by Newburgh,[14] and Worlidge.[15] Summer fruit was not kept above ten days or a fortnight. There was also some sort of agreement, among those who gave the

A loaded waggon ready to leave a Herefordshire orchard

matter thought, about what was going on inside the heap of apples that produced better cyder. It was observed that the piled fruit sweats a little, losing water but not the strength, sweetness or "spirits" of the apple. It followed that the quantity of cyder made after, say, six weeks, was smaller than that from fruit straight from the tree, and although occasional voices were raised against heaping the fruit because of the greater quantity and freshness of cyder straight from the tree,[16] there was almost unanimity in the seventeenth and eighteenth centuries about the advantages of maturing the fruit after picking. "The harsher the *Wild fruit* is, the longer must it lie on Heaps; for the same Fruit, suddenly ground, I have tasted good *Verjuice* [green and sharp apple juice]; being on heaps till near *Christmas*, all *Good-fellows* called it *Rhenish Wine*," as Beale observed.[17] What turned the verjuice into Rhenish wine was a process in the apple known variously as digestion, concoction or fermentation. Worlidge thought it was the destruction of a "Phlegmatic humour"[18] with the traditional qualities wet and cold (see above), and the apple as a result was lighter, warmer and drier. The "digestion" was also thought to break down the solid, fibrous parts of the apple, releasing more juice.[19] The essential qualities of the apple were concentrated in these processes, as is shown by Captain Sylas Taylor's reckoning: it took some thirty bushels of stored apples but only twenty bushels of apples direct from the tree, to make a hogshead of cyder. In other words the stored fruit was producing a bare quarter of its own volume in juice, given a hogshead of sixty gallons, usual at the time. In modern experience this is a low figure, and the juice must have been very strong. The point need not now be laboured that no water was added.

Nothing could better indicate that these cyderists were striving to make a rich and strong wine from their apples, and nothing could be a better guide to the modern cyderist. Most cyder fruit will keep from picking in November to pressing at Christmas. Even the soft and early varieties will do so in a cold autumn, although it is normally wiser to press them before they become too pulpy. The essential thing is to allow as much air as possible to circulate between the apples: if there is no space available under cover for shallow heaps on a dry surface, then the fruit can be kept in hessian sacks, as long as an eye is kept open for rottenness. Never use polythene bags, which retain the moisture and create ideal conditions for the growth of mould.

Grinding

Grinding the fruit presents perhaps the major difficulty for the small-scale modern cyderist. Anyone who plans to make cyder in large quantities must equip himself with a machine made for the purpose, unless he happens to live in one of the cyder counties and can use one belonging to a neighbour. It is still occasionally possible to buy mobile "mills" in auction sales: these are nineteenth-century devices with rotating blades, have generally been adapted to work from a tractor, and are known as "scratters" or "scratchers". It is even sometimes possible to buy a stone mill, but the problems of moving these any distance are considerable. This has not, unfortunately, prevented a large number of people from adopting the deplorable habit of erecting them, full of soil and geraniums, and in full view of the passing public, in modern front gardens.

Without a mill or scratter, the cyderist must choose an older or newer technology. We have seen early in this book that the medieval method of grinding apples was simply to "pound" or "stamp" them with a broad-ended piece of wood in a trough. It works; but it is hard work. In making real cyder, the greater number of apples to be processed calls for some sort of mechanical aid. It is possible to use a domestic electric mixer with a "liquidizing" attachment: these have rotating steel blades at the bottom of a glass container a quart or so in size. This readily reduces the contained apples to a pulp, but the process is slowed down by repeatedly emptying and filling the container. Nevertheless, with a little application it is surprising how soon a quantity of apples can be dealt with. Unfortunately for our purposes, these "liquidizers" work best with the addition of water; they also reduce the apples to very small particles, making it essential to use a very fine cloth for pressing.

Above A mobile "scratter" developed from the "Ingenio"

Below Two mobile presses and a horse-driven scratter

Another possibility is the old-fashioned mincer, turned by hand. If one can be found big enough to take the apples whole, so much the better. An important point is to make sure that all the metal parts of any device used to pulp apples are made of stainless steel, for ordinary steel will discolour and taint the cyder. This should be remembered, too, if the cyderist constructs some device of his own. He might, for example, want to take advantage of the power-tools now available.

Whatever contrivance is used, it is important to bear in mind that the purpose of grinding is *not* to reduce the apples to the smallest possible particles, which would produce a paste from which the juice could not be pressed, but to aim for a consistency roughly that of minced meat, with recognizable fragments of skin and tangible lumps of the flesh of the apple. Anything smaller will simply clog the pores of the cloth in the press.

A working stone horse-mill at Steps Farm, Checkley, Herefordshire

By whatever means he produces it, the mixture of solid and liquid parts of the crushed apple (no free juice is produced at this stage) is known as *pummice* or, to those with an eye open for a French derivation, *pomace*. It was also known as *murc*, or in Herefordshire today, *musk*. This terminology naturally spread to other parts of the equipment: in the horse-mill large and incompletely ground fragments of apple tend to collect on the rear-vertical inside face of the trough, in the space left by the wearing stones, and a "musking board" is used to bring these down to the floor of the trough. If the mill is big enough, the apples to be ground are kept in a pile on the flat area in the centre of the mill, whence they are "rowed down" with a "tammus" or "rowing down stick". The extent to which the pummice should be ground was a topic of dispute during the seventeenth and eighteenth centuries, and the arguments can be borne usefully in mind by the modern cyderist. It was often said[20] that excessive grinding in the stone horse-mill vitiated the cyder by crushing the pips and stems of the apples, which have a bitter taste. It was also argued that excessive comminution of the fruit released juices that added nothing to the quality of the final product. But when the maker stopped drinking his own cider, and sold the juice to a cider-dealer, there was every reason to grind as fine as possible and press as hard as possible, to extract the greatest quantity of juice. There are in fact good reasons for supposing that the juice that is most easily separated from the apple is the richest – leave it to the mills of God to "grind exceeding small".

Pressing – a plea for a vintage

The real art of cyder making lies in extracting the juice and in managing the fermentation. Here the modern cyderist may learn most from his predecessors of two and three hundred years ago and where he may indeed excel them. This art is in a sense a lost art, for there is no living tradition of making real cyder in England, no father-to-son teaching by example that connects us with those who discussed the best grafting stock for the Redstreak, or how crab-apple juice preserved perry from decay.[21]

But there is abundant evidence for us to be able to reconstitute the art from literary sources; with the benefit of historical hindsight we can see what the often empirically derived methods were striving for, and using modern techniques where necessary, we can refine, render more reliable and even improve these methods.

This is a plea for a vintage on a broad scale. Modern wine vintages are from the better vineyards in the better years: mixtures, poor vineyards and poor years make a non-vintage. Yet all this presupposes an unvarying technique with predictable results. The whole process of producing wine has become so refined that the only variables that control the quality of the product are those outside the power of man, principally the soil and the weather. But this sophistication of technique is, historically speaking, very recent. Bottling of wine was practised widely only in the seventeenth century, a period in which wine shared a history with cyder, watched over by people like Scudamore, who treated cyder as it should be treated – as a wine. A much greater degree of predictability (of quality) was introduced into the wine industry in France by the work of Pasteur in the later nineteenth century; only by then were the roles of yeast and micro-organisms recognized in the processes of fermentation and acetification of wine. But by then, too, cyder was all but ex-

Red streak

A seventeenth-century single-screw wooden cyder press. The barrel, positioned like a stund, is discharging into a gaun

tinguished in England, and there were no latter-day Scudamores to bring wine techniques to cyder.

So this plea for a vintage is no less than a plea to re-unite the histories of wine and cyder; to take up the lost history of cyder where it was put down in the early nineteenth century by the cider merchants and by the farmers who paid their men partly in water. Let us remove the uncertainties of technique so that it is the weather alone, as with wine, that declares a vintage. Then shall we claim, with Philips, that cyder is

> a wine delectable, that far surmounts
> *Gallic* or *Latin* grapes, or those that see
> The setting sun near *Calpe's* tow'ring height.
> Nor let the *Rhodian,* nor the *Lesbian* vines
> Vaunt their rich Must, nor let *Tokay* contend
> For sov'ranty; *Phanaeus* self must bow
> To th' *Ariconian* vales.[22]

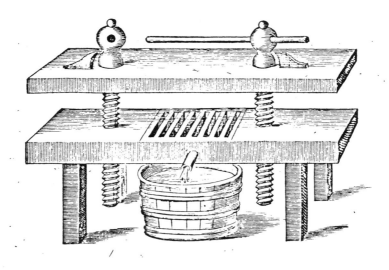

Above Worlidge's improved design for a cyder press, described in his *Two Treatises* of 1694. It was based on the oil-extracting press used by apothecaries, and had threads more closely spaced than usual

Below Another cyder press described by Worlidge. The suspended weights maintained a steady force on the "cheese" while the juice slowly emerged. This freed the operator for some other task

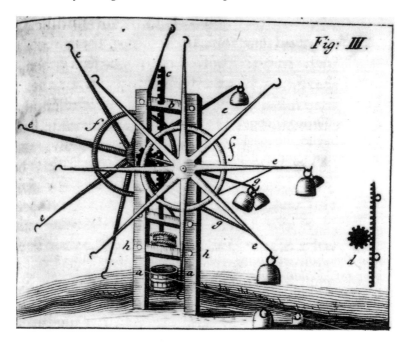

Fig: *III*.

The first step in re-establishing a vintage technique in cyder is to recognize the nature of the juice from the press. The murc from the mill is traditionally placed upon a cloth of horsehair placed on the stone base of the press. The cloth is then wrapped round and over the murc, and a second spread out on top and the process repeated. In this way a "cheese" is built up of several layers of murc in hair cloths, and a plate of wood being placed on top of the cheese, the press is screwed down. But before any

The large cyder presses of the eighteenth century were almost certainly based on the wine presses of the Continent. Compare screw-and-lever wine presses of the seventeenth and eighteenth centuries (e.g. *above* 1656) with the English cyder presses of the eighteenth century (e.g. *below*, 1747)

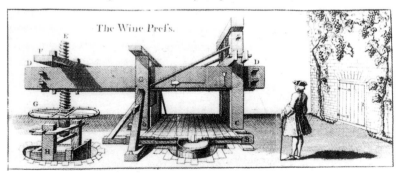

pressure is applied from the press, and shortly after the first hair cloth has been folded round the murc, juice spontaneously begins to run from the press into the collecting vessel. It is a bright brown in colour, thick, opaque and very sweet. It is from this that the very finest cyders of the seventeenth century were made. It was a technique consciously borrowed from France, where it was used in making wine. At the beginning of the seventeenth century Bacon had compared the habit of English cyderists of heaping up the apples to ripen them before grinding with the vine growers' habit of forcing bunches of grapes together to aid ripening;[23] by the second half of the century the natural comparison between the making of wine and the making of cyder led to the introduction of wine-techniques. Of these first runnings from the press, Worlidge says, "Which *Cider* so obtained, far exceeds that which is forc'd out; as the Wines of *France* that are unpressed, are by much preferr'd to those that are press'd"[24] and Sir Paul Neile tells us that "in divers *parts*, and even in *France*, they make *three* sorts of *Wine* out of one and the same *Grapes*",[25] the first without any pressure, the second and third (progressively more pigmented) with increasing pressure from the press. The method of separating this unpressed juice from the remainder was widely practised in Devon, where the large size of the presses, it is said,[26] allowed as much as a hogshead of juice to run off before pressing, to produce a highly valued cyder. Such cyder in Jersey sold at a premium of a crown a hogshead over that of "ordinary" cyder. Modern experience shows that, in contrast, the *last* turns of the press produce a thin, clear liquid without much colour and so low in natural yeast and sugar that it sometimes will not ferment without artificial encouragement.

The modern cyderist, then, has from his press a "must" that varies in sweetness from very to scarcely sweet. In producing a fine cyder he cannot of course retain only the first fraction and throw away the rest, and should aim to discover, by experiment and experience in the local situation, to what extent he can afford to dilute the sweetness of the first pressings by the addition of later pressings, without losing the slight residual sweetness that is necessary in a balanced final product.

At some point as pressing proceeds, he must decide that what

In the cider industry of the eighteenth century volume was more important than quality, and the huge presses were designed to extract the last drop, even though it had long been known that the quality of the expressed juice diminished in proportion to the effect used to extract it. Here we see that the principle of the lever has been added to that of the screw to develop a greater pressure. Such presses in Devon are said to have filled a hogshead in one operation

is now coming from the press cannot be allowed into his vintage. This later and weaker must should be treated as a modern equivalent of the "common cider" of the eighteenth century or of the "beverage" or "ciderkin" of an earlier period, not, indeed, by the addition of water, but in respect of its strength. It should, however, be treated as the *modern* equivalent of these drinks and its fermentation should be handled as described below, to produce a long drink for summer days.

It is not assumed of course that every modern maker of cyder has access to an old cyder press, but the process of pressing should present no real obstacle. Small fruit presses are available from manufacturers of home-made wine equipment, and a small wooden press operated, for example, by a hydraulic car jack, is not a difficult thing for a handyman to make. On this scale hessian or muslin is preferable to the coarse grained hair cloth of tradition, and net-curtains made of modern artificial fibre are remarkably strong.

In making a plea for a vintage, we have stepped ahead of some procedures that were thought essential by the old cyderists. Before the murc was pressed, it was commonly left in the mill, or in open vats, for a certain length of time. The purpose of this was to extend the process of concoction that had ripened the apple, the purpose that was also partly served by storing the fruit in heaps. It was central to seventeenth century thinking that the

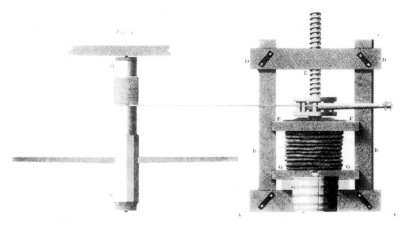

Another way of producing a more powerful press was to add a capstan to pull round the lever of a screw press

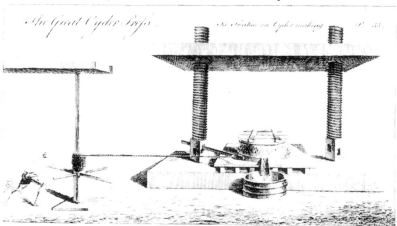

longer the necessary ripening concoction, the longer was delayed the concoction that ultimately turned the cyder into vinegar. Winter fruit needed all the concoction it could get, and correspondingly its cyder kept a great deal better than that of summer fruit, which was often not concocted after grinding but pressed straight away and drunk as soon as tolerably fine.

The modern cyderist would explain the better keeping qualities of the winter-fruit cyder in terms of its content of tannin and other principles. During the seventeenth century, a new development was taking place that greatly emphasized the difference between the long and short keeping cyders. This was the habit of bottling, borrowed from the wine-makers, and which is discussed below. Here we must note two important results of the

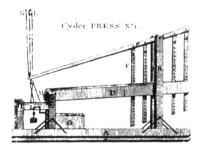 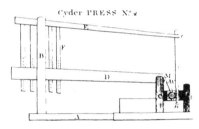

Yet another eighteenth-century way of developing great pressure was by the block and tackle (No. 1) or by the rack and pinion (No. 2) operating upon a pivoted lever, E, which is brought to bear on the descending arm of the press

habit: first, it emphasized the distinction between common cider, which was never bottled, and real cyder cultivated by Scudamore and those who followed him. Common cider and summer cider were drunk from the barrel in cider horns, which are no more than primitive drinking horns with a flat bottom, so that they will stand. Since the fermentation of such ciders ran uncontrolled into acetification, the barrel was tapped for drinking before fermentation had finished, and the opaque horns obscured the cloudiness of the cider. Real cyder, matured in bottle, was a sparklingly clear drink and the well-to-do cultivated the habit of drinking it from glasses specially made to enhance its brilliance.

Secondly, bottled cyder kept very much longer than that in the wooden cask, and this meant that much greater attention was given to processes that were thought to increase its longevity, like leaving the murc in the mill for a few days before pressing. In the earlier seventeenth century the most astringent and longest-keeping cyder was reckoned undrinkable in its first year and was normally drunk in its second or third year. Gradually the age of cyders increased with the adoption of bottling: seven years in the eighteenth century and twenty to thirty by the nineteenth.[27]

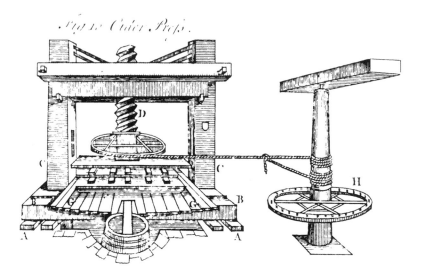

The parts of the press: this engraving, of the late eighteenth century, shows a capstan and single-screw press very much larger than those of the average farm or cottage. However, the essentials of the press (without the capstan) are the same in all cases. The wooden screw, D, is turned to develop pressure on the horizontal chuter board (at the level CC) between the two uprights. Between the chuter board and the chuter, G, the murc or pummice has been built up in layers of hair cloth, known as "hairs", into a "cheese" of about a dozen layers (not shown in the diagram). The juice runs from the chuter board into a wooden or stone container, the "cooler", before being transferred to the barrel

What was it, then, that happened to the milled cyder fruit, before pressing and being left open to the air, that contributed to its longevity and excellence? Worlidge, who bottled his cyder, tells us that in the murc, left standing for forty-eight hours,[28] a fermentation begins, and juice is transferred from the large particles. Moreover, by remaining on the ground skins of the apple (said Worlidge) the juice acquires a higher colour, much as rosé wines take the colour of the grape skins. Worlidge[29] had studied the apple under a microscope and concluded that the "pores" of the apple were much finer close to the skin: not only did these pores contain the ripest juice, being next to the sun-warmed skin, but, being fine, they were the most easily broken. Hence it was from these that the first, rich, unpressed juice flowed; Worlidge recommends, for a vintage, pressing the pared skin alone, or adding it to the pressed juice. The explanation of the changes that took place in the standing murc were taken from the science of the time: Worlidge, talking of the "digestion" or maturation of the hard fibres of the murc, was using traditional, vitalistic terminology that would have been intelligible to the ancients. Knight, experimenting in the first years of the nineteenth century, spoke of the uptake of "vital air" (oxygen) and the increase in specific gravity of the exposed murc, which he believed indicated an increase in its sugar content. Whatever *really* happens in ground apples left exposed for a couple of days, the modern cyderist will do well to follow the old method.

Fermentation

1. General It is, of course, the fermentation that turns apple juice into cyder. It is, therefore, the process that the modern cyderist should take the greatest care with. It is, fortunately, also a process that benefits immensely from modern knowledge. The historical evidence here is not so much a guide to action as an indication of aims that were being striven for, aims which we are now in a better position to achieve.

Historically, all the cyderists' efforts went into preventing the fermentation from going too far. There are two aspects to this. Firstly, it was part of the general attempt to preserve a slight sweetness in the final product to balance the native acidity and astringency of cyder; the other parts of this attempt were the devices resorted to in order to increase the sweetness of the unfermented must, described above. The second reason that a great deal of effort went into slowing down the fermentation was that no distinction was made between alcoholic fermentation, which turns apple juice into cyder, and acetification, which changes the alcohol in cyder into vinegar. Cyder was then simply an intermediate stage between the must and vinegar, and the techniques of cyder production were designed to lengthen the cyder stage to a period sufficient for its drinking.

2. Yeast No distinction was made between vinous and acetous fermentation because the latter seemed invariably to follow the former. It was not recognized until the later nineteenth century that the two processes depend on two different organisms, and in the seventeenth and eighteenth centuries it was widely disputed whether fermentation was a vital, chemical or even physical phenomenon. What happened in practice was that the expressed juice was left to ferment without any kind of preparation; when a knowledge of the part played by yeast became widespread, it was assumed that the "wild" yeasts present on the skin of the apples were responsible for the fermentation, and that the widespread vinegar bacteria soon infected the fermenting cyder. It seems in fact that it is the native yeast that grows on the apparatus used in making cyder rather than on the fruit, that is responsible for the fermentation.[30] That different sets of apparatus cultivate different strains of wild yeast no doubt accounts for the different cider produced by neighbours using the same fruit.

The modern cyderist cannot afford to rely on what chance supplies him with in the form of yeast. A greater danger is that vinegar bacteria will attack the alcohol as soon as it is produced, so that the apple juice appears to turn directly into vinegar without passing through the intermediate cyder stage. Probably real cyder is more prone to this accident than the modern descendant of seventeenth-century watered cider: it is conventional wisdom in Herefordshire today, and a strong reason for the

Most surviving single-screw presses have the screw and threaded socket of iron; in a number of cases this has clearly replaced the worn original wooden screw. This press has attractive "capitals" at the head of the side-timbers

A twin-screw press, probably of the early nineteenth century. The advantage of the two screws is not only in the greater pressure generated, but in its more even distribution. The stone base is of an unusual round shape

continuation of the traditional adding of water, that cyder made *without* water "won't keep". Indeed, sometimes it won't, *unless* the cyderist calls to his aid some modern help. Sulphur dioxide will kill off the vinegar bacteria and at least immobilize the native yeasts, leaving a more or less sterile must which can then be fed with a yeast of the cyderist's choice. A large range of wine yeasts are available to home wine-makers, and the difference between them (the type of wine they are used to produce) is less important than that they are all proper strains of *succhoromyces* and that the cyderist, and not chance, is in charge of the fermentation. On one important point, however, the cyderist differs from the maker of home-made wines. He is not, as they are, artificially concocting fermented sugar with various flavourings of vegetable origin, but is managing the fermentation of a drink as natural as *real* wine, and if he is anything of a purist he will not manipulate the contents of the must to achieve his result; that is to say, in aiming for the desirable slight residual sweetness in his cyder he will not be willing simply to add a bag or two of sugar before fermentation. It is true, of course, that sugar is added legitimately to some wines of areas of Germany where the sun will not produce enough sugar in the grapes, and that it is only by adding sugar that the alcohol level is raised to a point where fermentation ceases before the wine becomes entirely dry. The cyderist should aim for achieving a residual sweetness by choosing a yeast which has a *low* alcohol tolerance, not the high tolerance favoured by most home wine-makers. If he is willing to experiment, it is a very good idea to allow several small batches of cyder to ferment naturally. When the fermentation is over, the yeast can be extracted from any vessel that has produced a good cyder, and further cultivated by rapidly growing it in a solution of cane-sugar and yeast nutrient (from a home wine-makers' supplier). Such cultures will keep in a cool place until the cyder season comes round again. In *all* fermentations an airlock must be used, for this will keep infection out, and carbon dioxide, in which vinegar bacteria cannot grow, in.

3. Vessels The modern cyderist will normally have the choice of fermenting in wood or glass. The traditional method is to ferment in the wooden cask, but these vessels are becoming increasingly difficult to obtain with the adoption by brewers of the aluminium cask and with wine merchants abandoning the practice of shipping their wine in wood. Specialist home-made wine retailers sometimes supply small wooden barrels, and larger casks, of forty gallons or more, used to store sherry or spirits, can still be bought from one or two firms in London. Glass vessels of five gallons or so in capacity are not infrequently found, and smaller glass vessels are commonplace.

The type of vessel used, then, will depend largely on the amount of cyder to be made, but where there is a choice, the cyderist should be aware of the differences. Glass vessels have

The twin-screw press had many earlier applications. This is a
seventeenth-century example, of the sort used to press linen

the advantage of being easier to clean and sterilize and the progress of the fermentation may be watched. Wooden barrels are to a certain extent porous, and something like a third of the contents of a barrel will be lost by evaporation during the course of a year. The alcohol and water are the most volatile components of cyder, and are the major components of this lost third, so that the remaining two thirds is richer in the heavier, taste-forming components. This may not be a good thing when modern cyder fruit is bred to give adequate taste to a *long* drink and our modern cyderist is intent on squeezing the same ingredients into a smaller volume. What is very important with wooden casks, however, is that during this loss by evaporation the cyder *matures*. We have already noted a certain similarity between a high-tannin wine, such as claret, and a high-tannin cyder, like that made from White Beech, and such liquors may be too astringent to drink before maturation, but after a year or sometimes two in the wooden cask, are superior to many that were more agreeable when young. The "generous roughness" of the old Redstreak suggest that it was such a cyder, and in the eighteenth century some other cyders were noted as being drinkable only after the first or second year. Sometimes a claret is matured in a cask made of fresh oak for the purpose, and used once only, but such experience of the effect of the wood itself upon cyder is lacking. It is some combination of loss of volume and a slow inward diffusion of oxygen that accounts for maturation of cyder in the cask: on both counts the fermentation and storage of cyder in glass is quite different, but traditional knowledge of such differences is lacking, because cyder died out before glass fermenting vessels were introduced. Again, the cyderist should experiment, adopting as a premise the suggestion that astringent cyders do best in wood, the lighter, fresher cyders in glass.

4. Managing the fermentation The first step in any fermentation is to make sure the vessels are clean. Barrels and glass vessels should be thoroughly washed and then sterilized. This is best done with a solution of sodium metabisulphite, readily obtainable at chemists who handle home-made wine equipment. The metabisulphite is simply a convenient way of producing sulphur dioxide, which kills wild yeasts and vinegar bacteria. Sulphur dioxide is also produced by burning sulphur, and many of the old cyderists would burn a sulphur candle inside the cask to "sweeten" it, as we shall see below, while others used pepper, or quicklime. Half a dozen teaspoonsful of powdered sodium metabisulphite in half a gallon of water makes a good sterilizing solution, and it is as well to have it standing a little while in wooden casks, well corked and bunged.

The juice from the press, traditionally collected below it in a stone trough (it is unwise ever to allow cyder to come into contact with metal) is carried in a "gaun" to the cask, into which it is poured through a tundish or tunpail. When the vessel is full, the must should be treated at once with metabisulphite. The maximum dose in any circumstances (such as when the fruit was very "over-ripe", which in Herefordshire means anything up to black) is one *level* teaspoon per gallon. This will kill off everything in the must, but it is close to the level of tainting the resultant cyder. Once the fermentation is under way, not even this amount of metabisulphite will stop it, although it will reduce it to perhaps one hundredth of its former rate. Normally, half or, better, a quarter of a level teaspoon will produce a clean enough must for a dependable fermentation. (It is as well to level off the metabisulphite in the spoon with something flat; appearances are deceptive.) Following Pasteur's discoveries, metabisulphite is widely used in the French wine industry.

Having added the metabisulphite, two or three days should elapse before the yeast is added. A cork with an airlock should be used, to avoid possible infection of the cyder. It is now December or January in the cyderist's year, and the temperature in the cyder house is low. The fermentation is therefore slow to start and begins imperceptibly. The first sign is that the volume of the must increases, and it may rise through the airlock; then all the solid particles that can float are borne upwards on invisibly small bubbles to produce a froth like beaten white of egg, but yellow or brown in colour. This is the "flying lees" of the seventeenth century accounts, signifying the first stage in the cyder's purification of itself. This stage may be so vigorous that it will be best to remove the top cork or bung, replacing it as soon as possible.

Racking and maturing

As the weather gets warmer the cyder will begin to clear. A fermentation that began in juice pressed at Christmas will be on its way to completion by Easter. When the first signs appear of the cyder becoming clear it is necessary to rack it off into another vessel and dispose of the lees that have settled out of the fermentation. It is only necessary to rack off the cyder once, and it should be done before the fermentation has quite finished. If possible, fill the new cask up to the top, to prevent any collection of air, which would enable the vinegar bacteria to develop. If this is not possible, for example when the cyder has to be returned to the original vessel, the natural carbon dioxide from the still fermenting cyder usually suffices to form a blanket over the cyder and keep the bacteria at bay. Such cyder should be bottled earlier rather than later, as air is bound to get into the cask when fermentation ceases.

Maturation in cask and ageing in bottle are part of the mythology of wine-making lore. Neither had much importance before laying down of fine wines became widespread in the seventeenth and eighteenth centuries, and neither came to be applied extensively to the declining real cyder. The seventeenth- and eighteenth-century cyderist made no distinction between fermentation and maturation, but drank or bottled his cyder straight from the cask as soon as it was fit to drink: he knew that with some cyders he had to wait two or even three years, but this was in his eyes an extended fermentation. The improvement of cyder in the cask was doubtless an accidental discovery, probably when it was kept for long periods, for example on board ship as an antiscorbutic. In the middle of the eighteenth century it was noted with some surprise that cyder improved on an East India voyage.[31]

So, in producing a vintage, the modern cyderist cannot find a regular technique to emulate, developed by his predecessors, but he can, like them, borrow from the techniques of the wine makers of his time. Real cyder does improve from storage in a wooden cask, particularly if astringent. Light cyder, made at Christmas and racked at Easter, will keep in a cool place over the

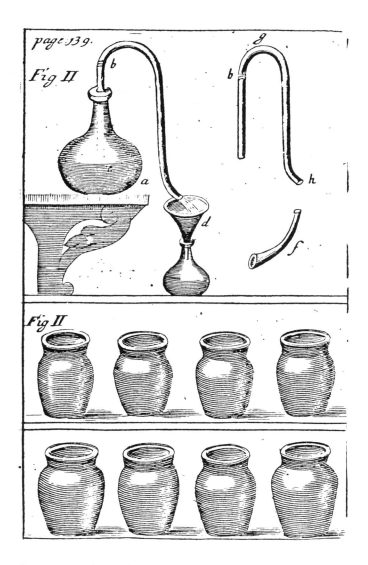

In preparing fine cyder it is necessary to rack the liquid from its lees. This was normally done by allowing the lees to settle below the tap in the barrel, but to achieve the greatest clarity in the racked cyder, Worlidge used glass fermenting vessels for better visibility. He also introduced the use of a glass tube to siphon the cyder from its lees with greater precision. These tubes were used by instrument makers in producing barometers, and Worlidge describes how they should be bent in a charcoal fire (1694).

summer for bottling in the autumn, and those with more astringency will keep twelve months longer. In the absence of a tested and tried tradition, the cyderist should again experiment; above all, a careful watch must be kept on the cyder in the wooden cask, where it is much more open to infection than in the bottle. In one important respect he cannot follow the procedures used to make red wines or still white wines. In the colder climate of England and with the extra sweetness of his must that the modern cyderist is looking for, the fermentation will be a drawn-out affair, continuing for many months and when the cyder has become almost clear. We shall see below that the aim should be to secure a very slight fermentation in the bottle to produce a slightly sparkling wine, and this should not be based on the addition of cane sugar, but on the natural sugars of the apple. In other words, the fermentation of at least a light cyder extends through the maturation period, and the modern cyderist, like his English predecessors, can here make no real distinction between fermentation and maturation. On the other hand, a very astringent cyder may have to be kept well beyond the end of its fermentation, when the cask *must* be kept topped up and tightly bunged. Such cyder can be treated as a still wine, or made *pétillant* in the manner described below.

Cider and pirkin

In arguing for a vintage, we have dealt with the process from the treatment of fruit to the beginning of the last stage, bottling. But there are times when one's sympathies with the eighteenth-century farmer, labouring at haymaking or harvest, became tangible in the need for a long, deep, cooling drink. Let anyone walk ten miles on a hot and dusty road, as G.K. Chesterton observed, and he will soon discover why beer was invented, an argument that applies equally to *draught* cider, not yet considered in this

The Forme of the Vessell

a - The Bung hole.
b - a small vent hole.
c - the Tap.   P. 100

The "stund", a vessel for the storage of cyder favoured by Worlidge and Taylor because the shape allowed the "leathern-coat" or skin on the top of the cyder to descend with the cyder in use without breaking. This was believed to help prevent contamination from the air. Barrels lying on their sides did not have these advantages and, without the use of special racks, were apt to roll, and could not be stacked one on another. The stund appears to be a vessel evolved uniquely for cyder during its seventeenth-century heyday

116

book. Moreover, we have seen that in selecting the best of his must for his vintage, the cyderist must put temporarily to one side the weaker last-pressing, ideal for a long cider.

For summer drinking, then, while the cyder is maturing in its cask, the cyderist should produce a lighter and longer drink, with a sparkle, to be tapped directly from the barrel. He may even wish to add water to the fruit in the mill, or he may be obliged to use water to grind the fruit in an electric mixer attachment. Whatever means he adopts to produce the must, it should be treated at first in the same way as his vintage, being sulphited and kept under an airlock. But the barrel should be tapped for drinking as soon as the cider is clear enough; it will never be entirely clear, and it is no use waiting.

The developing notion of fermentation

We have, for convenience, run straight through the techniques of cyder making without being diverted into looking at the beliefs and practices of two and three centuries ago. These beliefs and practices formed a tradition and development common to the production of wine; knowing about them may not help the modern cyderist to make better cyder, but it will help to fill the gap in the tradition caused by the disappearance of cyder.

The notion of fermentation was central to the concerns of the cyderist and wine maker. At the most empirical level he knew that the must "worked" and changed its nature, while at the most rational or scientific level the gentleman farmer would search among his acquirements in scientific or medical education for an explanation of what was happening. We have had occasion to remark before that during the centuries when real cyder was being made and enjoyed, the scientific view of the world was revolutionized. Natural philosophers increasingly sought explanations of the world and its contents in terms of inanimate particles in motion, so that the very human body itself became a machine, and it was even claimed that thought itself was a secretion of the brain as bile was a secretion of the liver. But it was mainly in late seventeenth-century France and Italy that the intellectual avant-garde was busy trying to prove that men were machines; in England there remained a stout scepticism about such new-fangled and godless ideas, and by the middle of the eighteenth century there was a widespread attempt to restore a soul and animated life to the human frame. But all of this was a battle of giants, and although the gentleman may have understood and shared in these intellectual fashions during his stay at university, we do not know how far down through society such knowledge filtered. It would be fanciful to suppose that the making of cyder was ever affected by Cartesian mechanism or Newtonian cosmology; but the people who wrote on cyder were educated in the fashion of their time, and sometimes put their scientific knowledge into action, or at least on paper, when dealing with cyder. In contrast, the country people who made cider were governed by a traditional technique, partly myth and partly accumulated rule-of-thumb experience. This tradition had considerable force, and part of it survives today, compelling the makers of cider to proceed in a certain fashion. Every generation makes some attempt to understand the rules of the traditional technique, but is unwilling to risk losing a hogshead by experiment. In other words the technique, as traditional, is strictly unintelligible, and modified only by accidental discoveries. An "intelligible" technique in contrast, would have been one that was modified according to the theoretical structure of the sciences (however fallacious to modern minds). The making of cyder, as a craft-technique, does show the occasional influence of theoretical science: some examples are given below.

In the whole theoretical dispute between those who believed in special life-forces in living things and those who would reduce everything to the physics of moving particles, there remained one curiously intractable problem, that of "fermentation". At the beginning of our period the word covered a range of phenomena in liquids and semi-liquid substances: the ebullition of alchemical reagents upon mixing, and putrefaction of organic fluids, as well as the brewing of beer and baking of bread. The role of yeast was necessarily recognized in the case of brewing and baking, and yeast was thought of as a "ferment", that is, an agent securing a specific change. But yeast was only one of a range of ferments, and the idea was elaborated by the Belgian Van Helmont in the first half of the seventeenth century: every change of substance, he said, had its own ferment, and ferments could produce their own substance out of water (which he demonstrated by adding nothing but water over a period of five years to a weighed willow tree growing in a pot).

Van Helmont's ideas represent a stage in scientific thinking when the doctrines of Aristotle and Galen were arousing some criticism, but before Western Europe had hit on the twin themes of atomism and mechanism as alternatives to Aristotle's essentially *biological* view of man and the natural world. The early cyderists were quite unaffected by the mystic and obscure doctrines of Van Helmont, which did not form part of science as taught in the universities and did not filter down to the craft level; but they did share an earlier, biological, view of the subject. Early writers like Markham[32] paid little attention to fermentation, because they were writing reports at second hand: for them juice is cyder as soon as it is in the barrel, allowing only for settling. Those with practical knowledge of making cyder all speak of fermentation as a process of cleansing, using the down-to-earth analogy of defecation. Nothing could be more biological than the idea of the cyder "purging"[33] itself by the precipitation of gross lees or faeces to the bottom of the cask and by the release of the "flying lees" or "feculancies" out of the upper bung-hole.[34] The expediency with which Worlidge urges the racking of the cyder (for which he introduced the use of a glass siphon) has as much to do with removing the cyder from its noisome deposit as preserving its sweetness by (he thought) slowing the fermentation.

The notion of fermentation as a purging away of a light and a heavy feculancy may possibly derive from Galen's analogy of the production of blood with the fermentation of wine, in which the light yellow bile and heavy black bile are ultimately directed to the intestines and expelled: every educated medical man would know of these ideas. The idea of the production of blood by a fermentive process was repeated in seventeenth-century terms by Thomas Willis, Sedleian professor of natural philosophy at Oxford, and his ideas were known to those of Evelyn's group who discussed the fermentation of cyder.[35] So at this level there is good evidence that the most modern scientific ideas of the time filtered down to those who made cyder, for Evelyn's *Pomona* was a practical guide.

Willis, Evelyn and their colleagues took a particularly English attitude to the revolution in science that was happening around them. The continental Cartesian mechanists were attempting to reduce the explanation of all natural change to a question of inanimate particles in motion. On the continent they largely succeeded, with three results that are of interest to us. Firstly the soul was denied a part in the workings of the body. Secondly, "spirits" of various kinds that were traditionally thought to exist in organisms were reduced to passive materiality. Thirdly fermentation, the most characteristically biological change, was reduced to physics. These new ideas did not convince the English. A general piety, not antagonized by a doctrinaire Church, ensured the retention of the idea of a soul, not only as an agent of personal immortality but in a traditional way as a force in the workings of the body. Spirits retained something of their traditional role as subtle and self-active substances, fine enough to communicate with the immaterial soul and active enough to impose motion on matter. Now arose the ambiguity that still attends the word "spirit" in the English language, a word meaning both a semi-animate self-mobile substance approaching immateriality, and a chemical essence. Willis's use of the term includes both senses in the single context of the human body.

It was the "spirit" of cyder that was revealed by fermentation. The word has its English meaning of a subtle but powerful self-active substance: it will burst wooden casks if too tightly confined, even by the "skin" that grows over the fermenting cyder,[36] and will blow corks from their bottles. It seems often to have been believed that the spirit was not produced by fermentation, but revealed by it as the cyder cleared itself; some thought that spirit itself caused the fermentation[37] and the technique of reducing the fermentation was then to allow evaporation of spirit by exposing the cyder to the air. Others believed that fermentation was caused by the heavy lees, and that the spirit was a product, so that the excellence of the fruit could be measured by the volume of spirit produced by distilling the cyder:[38] Beale reckoned a pint of spirit from a gallon of cyder.

So, the lees and the spirit of cyder were thought to be either the cause or the result of fermentation, and their removal from the bulk of the cyder was generally reckoned beneficial, by purging it of impurities or slowing down the fermentation before the loss of all the sweetness. Different techniques were employed at different stages of the fermentation to achieve these ends. To begin with, the habit of sweetening the barrels by burning sulphur inside them was extended to the first stages of fermentation by pouring in the must immediately. Burning sulphur, then called brimstone, produces sulphur dioxide, just as metabisulphite does in water: the latter technique is simply a convenient way of achieving the aims of the first, from which it is derived. The use of brimstone is another technique borrowed from the production of wine[39] by the seventeenth-century cyderists; Worlidge, with great efficiency, drew the fumes of burning brimstone through a pipe into the hogshead, "by which means the *Cider* is impregnated with the spirit of *Sulphur*, which will give it no alteration, save only for its salubrity and duration".[40] Brimstone also had the advantage of slowing the fermentation: Stafford[41] in the eighteenth century recommended burning a mixture of brimstone, burnt alum and wine brandy together with nutmegs, cloves and coriander for this purpose, and Knight in the nineteenth century used a similar method. Another technique employed for these purposes was that of aiding the clarification of cyder by encouraging "defecation" of its lees. A traditional method of doing this was to add fresh blood[42] at the rate of a quart per hogshead.[43] Perhaps this is an origin of one of the curious myths of cyder making, namely that cyder is improved by hanging a piece of meat in the barrel: the cyder is said to gain quality as the meat disappears. A practice that was tolerated as late as the early part of this century in parts of Gloucestershire was to leave the upper bung-hole of the vessel open after the fermentation had thrown off the "flying lees". In the sticky mess left by the subsiding lees on the outside of the barrel near the hole, the footprints of rats would be seen approaching, but never returning from the open hole. Their bones alone survived the action of the cider, to be washed out when the barrel was finally cleaned.

Another curious myth of cyder making is that the cyder increases in strength during the period of maturation. Captain Sylas Taylor held that the Redstreak, scarcely edible as a fruit, gave cyder that was drinkable after six months and "dangerously strong" after three years.[44] Beale observed that cyder preserved in bottles "does almost by time turn to *Aquavitae*; the *Bottles* smoak at the opening, and it catches *flame* speedily, and will burn like *Spirit* of *Wine*, with a fiery taste".[45] Worlidge thought bottled cyder approached the strength of Canary wine in time. During the maturation of cyders like the Foxwhelp and Bromsbury Crab, which were thought undrinkable before two years had passed[46] great care was taken to preserve the skin that formed on top of the cyder, and which protected it from the air. In Devon it was the habit to throw dust or wheat chaff on top of the cyder to thicken this coat, and Worlidge recommended wheat grains.[47] Worlidge also used, in a vertical position, a straight-sided vessel known as a "stund"[48] to lessen the strain on the "*Leathern-Coat*" on top of the cyder as it descended, with use, through the vessel. Newburgh thought that the strength of a matured cyder was owing to this coat preventing the loss of spirit.[49]

Bottling

Bottling was the last essential step in producing the great cyders of the seventeenth and eighteenth centuries. It also is a vitally important step for the modern cyderist in his pursuit of excellence in a revived cyder tradition. The modern purposes of bottling are to improve the cyder through its ageing in the bottle, and to preserve it for a much greater length of time than is possible in the wooden cask. The habit of bottling was probably first employed simply to preserve the cyder, and was borrowed by Lord Scudamore and Evelyn's correspondents from the wine trade, where, in the seventeenth century, the habit was becoming widespread, although probably more for the convenience of retail distribution than for the benefit accruing to the wine. The same reason determined that bottled cyder played a large part in the eighteenth-century English cyder trade. Similarly, at first, individuals bottling cyder for their own consumption were more concerned with the preservation of their cyder than in its improvement in "laying down".

But bottling cyder has one advantage which may not have been borrowed from the wine trade, and which may therefore be part of the independent tradition of English cyder: the cooler climate of England and the longer fermentation of cyder meant that often a gentle fermentation within the bottle produced a *sparkling* wine upon uncorking, even after a number of years. This was no sooner recognized[50] than eagerly sought after, and it should remain the goal of the modern cyderist. During this late stage of the fermentation the cyder throws down a deposit in the bottle and becomes perfectly clear, in a way that never happens in the barrel.

Before the cyder is bottled, it should be blended. The modern cyderist will do well to ferment separately each of his varieties of fruit, so that he may find by experience which best suits his palate and his soil. He may find that for his vintage the juice of no single variety has the proper balance of astringency, sweetness and other elements of taste, and that such a balance must be achieved by mixing the cyder of several varieties.

Such a mixture should be left in the cask for a while to make sure that a vigorous fermentation does not recur – often the residual sweetness of one cyder, although stable, will promote a fermentation when added to another cyder. Indeed the whole art of bottling cyder is to decide upon the proper moment to do so, when the fermentation is imperceptible but not absolutely complete. If it is bottled too soon the fermentation in the bottle breaks it, or produces "pot-gun drink"[51] that shoots from the bottle; if bottled too late it will be flat and uninteresting. The best time to bottle is in the autumn, when the fermentation has run through the summer, although some of the old writers, seeing the clarity of the cyder and its quiescent fermentation in cold weather, recommended bottling in March.[52] But these bottles had to be kept very cold throughout the ensuing summer to avoid excessive fermentation: they were even kept in running water. It was of course the "spirit" of the cyder that give it its briskness in the bottle, and the art of the cyderist was to achieve the right "temper" or balance of the spirit and the liquid in the bottle, "For the right *temper* of *Bottle-Cider* is, that it *mantle* a little and *sparkle* when it is put out into the glass".[53] The safest way of achieving the right "temper" was, and is, to allow the fermentation to finish completely, and then to add a known quantity of sugar to the cyder before bottling. Sometimes raisins were added for the same purpose, sometimes a knob of white, or "loaf", sugar the size of a walnut or nutmeg.[54]

Here the native English tradition of cyder making was at its height; while the idea of bottling it seems to have come from France in the time of Charles I with Lord Scudamore, who bottled *his* cyder, yet the improvement of cyder in bottle, and more particularly the development of a mature sparkling wine, appear to be independent of the Continental wine tradition. Bottling and laying down *wine* in England did not begin until the late seventeenth century,[55] a long time after Scudamore, and in the intervening period the cyder and wine traditions separated. This separation was initiated by Cromwell's Navigation Act of 1651, which was designed to destroy Dutch trade in English ports. Dutch ships had carried almost all the wines imported from the Rhine and Moselle, and a great deal of that coming from France, and so the Act was disastrous for the import of foreign wines. This made the nation acutely aware of its dependence on wines from abroad, and this, combined with the economic arguments we have already met, concerned with currency going abroad and the need to preserve grain for bread rather than brewing, formed the background to the efforts made after the Restoration by Evelyn and others in the Royal Society to establish cyder as a national wine. By the early 1680s the import of French wine had practically ceased, and although the upper classes turned increasingly to Portuguese and Levant wines, the heavy taxation on these imposed by the Wine Act of 1688 was an added reason for the continued development of the native cyder.

The absence of French and German wines not only meant that people turned to cyder in their place, but that they were cut off from the habit of producing a sparkling wine. Wine was shipped in the wood, and normally transferred from the barrel to the table as required in a bottle. The process of producing a *sparkling* wine was necessarily conducted at the *destination* of imported wines, now absent. "Champagne" as the name of a sparkling wine did not enter the language until the later seventeenth century. The independent tradition of making an English sparkling wine, cyder, continued through the eighteenth century. The Methuen Treaty of 1703 imposed another heavy tax on French wine, and encouraged the import of port from Oporto and Lisbon, in addition to the *vin du pays* of Portugal that were already popular. The technique of producing a sparkling wine was kept alive while cyder was drunk, but died in the nineteenth century when common cider alone survived the re-introduction of wines from abroad.

A word should be said here about the habit of laying down wine. The practice is said[56] to date from the last quarter of the eighteenth century when were first introduced the modern form of cork and the shape of bottle we know now, which allows a number to be stacked on their sides. Undoubtedly the habit was found very useful in the case of fortified and durable wines like port, but the technique was already more than a century old among the cyderists, and like the simple act of bottling, it may have been used for cyder before wine. The habit is a natural development of corking a bottle securely to condition the cyder to obtain a sparkle in the glass, which was looked for by Scudamore and his English followers. The manner of sealing the bottle was therefore important; the seventeenth-century wine bottle, broad-based to stand securely on the table (and not to be stacked on its side) was stopped merely with a peg of wood on its short journey from barrel to the table. The early cyderists therefore looked around for better seal. Worlidge[57] recommended glass stopples for cyder bottles, each to be ground to a perfect fit with a paste of emery powder and oil. He recognized, however, the danger of such a perfect fit causing the bottles to burst if the cyder was bottled when still too sweet, and to avoid this, good quality cork was to be used. Robert Hooke of the Royal Society had already described the microscopical appearance of cork, with its many "cellular" cavities, which were thought to make it slightly porous, allowing the escape of excessive "spirit" of cyder.

It was the practice among the cyderists of Worlidge's time to keep their bottles, awkwardly shaped for stacking, on shelves or in a frame, but always in a horizontal position, so that the corks were kept moist by the contents in order to lessen the communication between the external air and the enclosed spirit. The habit was more than a trick to preserve and condition the cyder and was "laying down" in the modern sense to improve the wine. We have seen above that the seventeenth-century cyderists thought the strength of bottled cyder increased, and it was generally thought, in Worlidge's words, "Drawing of *Cider* into Bottles, and keeping it in them well stopt for some time, is a great improver of *Cider*".[58] Beale said of old Redstreak cyder "in *Bottles* and *sandy Cellars* [it] keeps the *Records* of late *Revolutions* and old *Majoralities*".[59] The important thing was to keep the bottles in a constant and low temperature. They were buried in sand, and kept in running water; Worlidge advised the building of vaults at the bottom of a well. By the middle of the nineteenth century Herefordshire cyder was reckoned to keep twenty to thirty years, that of Devon about five.[60]

Faults and their correction

The modern cyderist should encounter far fewer difficulties than his predecessors. He understands the causes of fermentation and acetification and above all he always has available his sodium metabisulphite. Nevertheless, things can go wrong, particularly if experimental techniques are being employed. Additionally, even if there is nothing wrong the final product may lack some quality which a little adjustment can put right.

The most frequent fault will be that the cyder turns out to be too dry, perhaps from lack of sufficient sugar in the must. This dryness produces an unpleasant hard taste, excessively astringent, which completely masks the potential of the cyder. The best way to treat this is to forget about bottling and produce a cyder to be drunk from the cask. Rack the dry cyder from its lees into a new cask, and add sugar (dissolved in water) at a rate of a bag (1 kilo: 2.2 pounds) to six gallons. It is essential to wait about a week while the cyder conditions itself by means of a gentle fermentation, and then it should be drunk without delay, as the fermentation proceeds. If freshly pressed must is available, it can be used in place of sugar, as Worlidge used it in the cask and in bottle.[61]

Other faults possible in cyder are excessive astringency and acidity, owing to the preponderance of natural taste elements, and acetification, resulting from infection. A clear distinction was not always made between astringency, acidity and sourness, and many remedies were addressed to a common problem. The addition of unground wheat grains was a common remedy for "sour" or "acid" cyder. Ellis[62] records that a pint of wheat in a hogshead was held to sweeten and feed the cyder; Worlidge recommends a gallon to the hogshead to correct acidity; Newburgh specifies half a peck to ameliorate "harsh and eager" cyder, terms usually signifying an acetous state; Dr Smith prescribes a quart of wheat per hogshead as a matter of course for all cyder expected to keep two years or more, and Knight says that wheat or toast will prevent acetification.

Worlidge, at least, distinguished between acidity and sourness, or acetification, and besides wheat for the cure of the former, he recommends two or three eggs, or a pound of figs to be added to the hogshead. Newburgh, who borrowed these ideas, had a less clear understanding than Worlidge, and believed the wheat increased the fermentation, and the eggs and figs would recover a cyder from a vinegary state. Sometimes mustard was added to the cyder, to correct a musty flavour, to increase the fermentation,[63] to clarify the cyder or to preserve it.

Of these remedies, the modern cyderist may well experiment

with wheat and will come to little harm if he uses mustard. He will need to be a little braver, perhaps, to add eggs to his cyder, and he would be foolhardy experimentally to determine the truth of the myth that a piece of meat adds body to cyder. In fact, most of the common faults of taste can be masked by the judicious use of sugar, and continuous sampling should warn the cyderist if the fermentation is in danger of becoming acetous. At the slightest vinegary taste, the must should be treated again with sodium metabisulphite, at an absolute maximum rate of one level teaspoonful per gallon. This will stop the acetification and reduce the fermentation to the merest fraction. It is as well to drink the cyder as soon as the sulphur dioxide has cleared and the cyder begins to come back into condition. Excessive acidity can be treated with pharmaceutical calcium carbonate.

The homely remedies of Worlidge and the seventeenth-century cyderists were designed to enable the farmer or gentleman to rescue his cyder from disaster and make it possible for him to drink it. In contrast, much of the advice offered in the next century is aimed at the trade, at the cider merchants who needed every sophisticated trick to maintain the price of a basically unsound cyder, and to add body and flavour to the thin cider made by watering the purchased must. Apart from sugar and raisins, shavings of fir and spirit of turpentine were used to restore an "impoverish'd" cider.[64] Acetous cider was ameliorated with brick-powder and alum; poorly flavoured cider was treated with honey and spices: cloves, cinnamon, ginger, "zedoary", "orras root" and "grains of paradise". "Ropy" cider, which has a slimy feel,[65] was treated with burnt alum, lime, chalk, plaster, "Spanish white", and "adding to these the flour of Beans and Rice, each a quart, beating them well together with the Cyder, blow off the froth and cover the bung-hole with a clean tile".[66] Often enough coarse sugars or molasses were added to colour the cider, and sometimes distilled spirits were added to increase its strength.

Part Three

Reproduction of a painting *The Cider Mill* by E. Borough Johnson (1867–1949)

We have now looked at the history of real cyder and at the techniques of making it; it might now seem superfluous to offer advice to the patient and thirsty cyderist on what to do with it when made. But often he will have cyder in wood that will not keep for leisurely drinking, or that which has given of its best in blending: such cyder will form an agreeable basis for other drinks, and can be extensively used in cooking. If he needs an excuse to entertain his friends, what better reason than food and drinks made to recipes two or three hundred years old?

The labourer in the fields at harvest, with his costrel of cider

Drinks – general

Cyder not only adds its own characteristic taste to drinks, but allows the flavour of other components to appear more strongly. Some of the substances in herbs and flowers are soluble in alcohol, but not in water, and are thus transferred to the palate more readily in drinks like cyder. This principle is used medically in the making of tinctures, and was known to the seventeenth-century cyderists. Worlidge tells us that cyder is "the most proper Vehicle to transfer the vertues of many *Aromatick* and *Medicinal Drugs, Spices, Fruits, Flowers,* etc".[1] He gives four principal medical plants to be used in this way: juniper, ginger, rosemary and wormwood. Rosemary and wormwood were already commonly given in a preparation with wine[2] and wormwood came to be used extensively in vermouth, juniper in gin and other herbs in the monastic benedictine. Worlidge's four plants were not chosen randomly, but according to their basic qualities. We have seen above that all food and drink was supposed, in traditional medicine, to act upon the body according to its predominant Quality, whether Hot, Dry, Cold or Moist. Cyder was considered Cold, likely to damage the power of digestion, which depended on natural heat, and Worlidge has chosen plants that are all Hot and Dry, to counterbalance the effects of cyder in the body. Contemporary theory established four Degrees of each Quality, so that the medical man could gauge the intensity of the effect. Culpeper tells us that wormwood is hot and dry in the first degree, that is, as warm as the warm humour of the body, blood. As a plant governed by the planet Mars, wormwood was a general preserver of health, and in particular helped to expel choler. Ginger was hot and dry in the second degree, and so helped digestion; juniper was hot in the third degree and was considered an excellent all-round antidote to poisons, animal and insect bites, and plague.

Apart from specifically medical plants used in cyder, there were a few herbs employed for other purposes. Clary, *salvia sclarca*, is a pot herb cultivated since at least the Middle Ages in English gardens, and often used to make clary wine. "Clary water" in the eighteenth century was a mixture of brandy, clary flowers and cinnamon. The flavour of clary leaves or flowers was strong enough to ameliorate the rough cyder of Devon, and is said to have made it taste like Rhenish wine.[3] The seeds or leaves are said by Culpeper[4] to give wine aphrodisiac powers.

Herbs can also be added to cyder cup with great effect, and those who like growing herbs will enjoy experimenting with them. Rosemary is sometimes added to cyder in Herefordshire, and can be used also in recipes that involve mulling the cyder. Borage is an excellent herb for a summer drink – again, allow the finely chopped leaves to stand for a little while in the cyder, before adding slices of cucumber and ginger ale. A little mint or a piece of orange peel does not come amiss. Obviously the amount of the ingredients should be altered according to the acidity, astringency and sweetness of the cyder. A little sherry or even port will add body.

To give extra flavour and colour to cyder, Worlidge recommends the addition of various kinds of fruit juice, all of which would certainly make an attractive drink for the modern cyderist to try. Elderberries are much recommended for this purpose, and were widely used by dishonest wine merchants to "stretch" port and red wines. We can agree with Worlidge that currants, raspberries, blackberries and mulberries provide agreeable juice to add to cyder; for example as the basis of a punch. The practice of adding mulberry juice to the juice of the cider fruit seems to have been begun by a Mr Samuel Colepress, who wrote to the editor of the Royal Society's journal about it in 1667. "Cyderseason approaching," he observed, "I know not how to conceal from the delicate and curious cyder-drinker ... the notice of a liquor as commendable as yet rare. It is a composition of the Juyces of good cyder-apples and Mulberries, producing the best tasted and most curiously coloured liquor, that many either saw or tasted."[5]

Cyder cups as long, cooling drinks are very pleasant in the summer. Take advantage of the strength of real cyder to draw out the juices of the fruit: slice oranges, lemons, apples and melons, either separately or in the same drink, and let them stand for a while in the cyder, in a cool place. Add a little sugar or honey if the cyder is too dry. Before serving add enough soda water or ginger ale to give a sparkle to the drink. Fresh or frozen soft fruits can also be used – raspberries freeze very well, and yield a good juice in the cyder cup; and what could be better than fresh strawberries, added in slices?

A number of warming drinks for winter evenings can be made with cyder. The general principle is to add spices and sugar and to heat the mixture. A number of different spices can be used, like mace, ginger and coriander but cinnamon and cloves are indispensable. The object is to produce a short rather than a long drink, and real cyder, heavier and stronger than common cider, is much more suitable. When a proper balance of sweetness and spice has been found for the cyder at hand, add a little port or brandy.

Some seasonal recipes for drinks

In looking for different recipes for drinks, the cyderist must bear in mind the season of the year. Not only will long, cool drinks be more attractive in the summer than the winter, but the condition of the cyder available will vary with the season. Any new season's cyder that will not make a vintage should be used as a fresh, fruity mixer for drinks as soon as the weather warms up and the cyder is tolerably fine. Correspondingly the autumn and winter are the seasons to make use of end-of-barrels, cyder that has contributed to, but not fully used up in, blending, or that which has been left to mature in the wood for a season. Such cyders are often eccentric, strong and even tending to be acetous in taste and are best used with spices and other components of strong or hot mixtures. In contrast, bottled vintage cyder does not vary through the season in the same way, and can be used as the basis of summer and winter drinks. Often it will be the only cyder available in the spring and early summer, before the new season's fermentation is complete.

SPRING

Worlidge's Warmer

Spring weather before the new fermentation has finished is rarely warm enough to demand a long, cooling drink, and this is the time to try the traditional "heating" spices. For every bottle of sparkling vintage cyder, take a dozen dried juniper berries and a piece of root ginger roughly equal to the berries in volume. Bruise the berries and ginger in a little old cyder, or, if the weather is even worse than the usual English spring, brandy, and leave for half an hour. Press the berries and ginger, and remove. Add the newly uncorked cyder and serve.

Woodruff Cup

Wild woodruff, *Asperula odorata*, should be gathered in May. Put a handful into a jug and cover with cyder – a still cyder will do, perhaps some that has kept in the wood from a previous season. Taste frequently to make sure the woodruff is not too strong. Add a dry sparkling vintage cyder – the same volume as that already used – and serve.

This was originally a German recipe, the Mai Bowle, using Palatinate wine to absorb the flavour of the herb, and champagne to give the sparkle. Champagne is extremely effective in mixtures of this kind – some are described by Robin McDouall,[6] who describes the Mai Bowle as the "most wonderful German spring drink" – but few of us can afford to experiment with champagne in this way, and a dry vintage cyder is an excellent substitute. Perhaps surprisingly, a dry light mead, made from a pale honey such as alfalfa or a light English honey, comes close to champagne in taste when bottled properly to preserve its sparkle, and served cold. Producing mead would be the subject of another book, and we must be content here to observe that what it lacks in fruitiness is supplied very well by mixing it with cyder.

Ascorbic Scrumpy

No one today suffers from scurvy after a winter without fruit and vegetables, at least to the extent that the medieval peasant or the eighteenth-century sailor did. But the body can usefully absorb ten times the amount of vitamin C that is necessary to prevent scurvy and the amount rises in illness; so a little over and above our normal intake can be beneficial. The fruit juice richest in the vitamin is blackcurrant (three times as much as orange juice and nine times that of lemon juice), which is an excellent component of cyder drinks.

Use cold bottled vintage cyder with a good sparkle, or Symonds' Scrumpy Jack straight from the bottle, and pour on to three or four tablespoons of a proprietary blackcurrant drink in a pint mug. Drink, relax and think of the scurvy you have avoided.

A drink at haymaking in 1806; an etching by William Pyne

SUMMER

Drinks for the summer should be longer than those of other seasons, that is, they should contain less alcohol for a given volume to allow the thirst to be quenched without making the drinker tipsy. All good generalizations have good exceptions, and this has an excellent one: Black Velvet, known to the Victorians as "Bismark". This is properly a mixture of equal quantities of Guinness and champagne, served very cold, but cider has long been a cheaper substitute, and our cyderist will find that a dry vintage cyder will do very well.

By summer the new season's cyder will be becoming drinkable from the barrel, and will have lots of the sparkle that is necessary for summer drinks. However, it will not have enough to add sparkle to a flat drink, so where the recipe demands it, use soda water or bottled tonic water or perhaps bitter lemon. Then the cyder can be used to extract the flavours of fruits by steeping. In the strawberry season, slice a pound of strawberries fairly finely, add sugar and ice and allow to stand in half a gallon of cyder from the barrel for at least an hour. Then add some fizz in the shape of soda water and, if you can afford it, three or four glasses of an orange-flavoured liqueur.

The same principle can be used with other fruits. Try a pound of raspberries (honey can be used to sweeten them, but do not use too much) and again allow to stand in half a gallon of cyder. Add soda water until the drink is alive, and perhaps a little extra flavour with a liqueur like kirsch.

There is a general principle that cyder goes very well with fruit, so that cups made with apples, peaches, apricots and so on, including melons, all cut rather small, seem to add something to the taste of both the cyder and the fruit. Fruit juices are available, sometimes in a concentrated form, in tins, bottles and frozen, and these will form an excellent basis for a cyder cup. Apple juice, orange, lemon, grapefruit, the taste of each carried over by the cyder, sweetened to taste with sugar or honey, brought alive by soda water, ginger ale or lemonade, perhaps with a zest of lemon, a sprig of mint or a few crushed leaves of borage: the list of possible combinations is endless, and the cyderist will soon discover his favourites.

AUTUMN AND WINTER

Cyder-Royal

We cannot make cyder-royal according to the patent of Richard Haines in 1684 because the law forbids us to distil alcohol. His method was to distil one hogshead of cyder and add the spirit to another; but he also observes that brandy may be used with propriety in place of distilled cyder, and on a small scale we can reproduce Haines's recipes for brandy and cyder cocktails.

For a basic cyder-royal, add a double brandy to rather less than a pint of cyder, sweetened with sugar. Haines recommended spicing the mixture with a little bruised coriander seed in a linen bag, and the addition of wormwood was said to be an aid to digestion.

Like Worlidge and Digby, Haines gave some attention to the country wines that were being made in his day. *"Royal-Currant*

Wine" is the wine of currants (probably red, and not dried currants) fortified with a distilled spirit of the same wine – in our case brandy – at the rate of one volume of spirit to eight volumes of wine, together with a little sugar. "Wine-Royal" of gooseberries, cherries and mulberries is made in the same way in each case, and each is worth trying. Haines's purpose was to make the ordinary cider and country wine of his day as rich as Canary wine; and it is worth remembering that port as we drink it today is the result of a very similar idea – to enable the local wines of Portugal to travel safely to England by the addition of brandy to fortify, enrich and stabilize them. Indeed, Haines makes much of the keeping qualities of cyder-royal, and advises us to keep the mixture in the wood to mature: by this, he explains, the "Chilly, Cold Phlegmatic part of the Cyder" will be balanced by the strong, warm and lively spirits, to make an enduring liquor so wholesome that "'tis so farr from Clogging the Stomach, or Clouding the Brain with thick muddy vapours, that I do believe a man may (WERE IT NOT A SIN) be Fuddled and Sober two times in a Day with this Liquor, without mischief to his Health".

Bishop

Unlike the ephemeral mixed cups of summer drinking are one or two traditional winter drinks which have borne the same name for a long time – "Bishop" was a warm drink of wine, sometimes with sugar and water, together with an orange, in the early eighteenth century, and in the early nineteenth century the orange was commonly roasted.[7] Here is a recipe published by Robin McDouall: rather than reduce the strength of the port by burning, dilute its volume with cyder.

Make several incisions in the rind of a lemon. Stick cloves in these and roast the lemon by a slow fire. Put small but equal quantities of cloves, mace and allspice with a trace of ginger into a saucepan with a ½ pint of water. Let it boil until it is reduced by a half. Boil one bottle of port wine, burn a portion of the spirit out of it by applying a lighted paper to the saucepan. Put the roasted lemon and spices into the wine, stir it up well, and let it stand near the fire for 10 minutes. Rub a few knobs of sugar on the rind of lemon, put the sugar into a bowl or jug, with the juice of half a lemon (not roasted), pour the wine into it, grate in some nutmeg, sweeten it to your taste and serve with lemon and spice floating in it.

Mulled cyder

Cyder mulled with sugar and spices in a tin or copper "devil" is a traditional winter drink. The principle is the same as that of mulling red wine; that is, the astringency and acidity of the drink, which might be excessive when it is hot, are balanced by the addition of sugar or honey, and the warming qualities of the drink are accentuated with spices. Real cyder is much closer to red wine in its astringent qualities than is ordinary cider, but somehow the ancient quality, attributed to cyder, of "coldness" survives all but the best attempts to turn it into a warming winter drink. It is best mixed with a strong red wine in about equal measures: add a glass of brandy or other liqueur to every pint of the mixture, two lumps of sugar, three or four cloves, and a small piece of cinnamon. Bring to the boil and immediately remove from the heat. Strain and serve.

Possets and syllabubs

Real cyder also presents the opportunity of reviving some old English drinks. Posset was a peculiarly English drink, unknown in France, and enjoyed during the heyday of English cyder. Posset and syllabub were often identical, and it was only by the eighteenth century that "syllabub" could mean, more precisely, a light, frothy dish to be eaten with a spoon. The original method of making possets and syllabubs was to curdle fresh milk (preferably directly it had come from the cow) with a fruit acid or alcoholic drink. Possets were made with ale and wines, and syllabubs additionally with cyder, often so acid as to be "verjuice" or the juice of green or crab-apples. The mixture was whipped as the cyder as added, sweetened and often spiced.

The modern cyderist should perhaps adopt the eighteenth-century distinction and enjoy both posset and syllabub, the latter whipped up with cream, sugar and cyder, while posset can be enjoyed as a warm, spiced, cyder-and-milk. Hot posset was regarded as an excellent remedy for colds, while cyder-syllabub, like all cyder, was held to cool the stomach, particularly in choleric people.

A verjuice press. Verjuice is the sharp juice of crabs or other apples, sometimes fermented and sometimes not; the term was often applied pejoratively to cyder that had become acid in fermentation (today known as "squeal-pig" cider). Its acidity is useful in making syllabubs and possets. Large quantities were not required, and the verjuice was often pressed from the fruit by the simple rotating action of this roller-press

Possets were often made with sack, a white wine from Spain and the Canaries. Sir Kenelm Digby gives a number of recipes where sack can be replaced by "muscadin", a white wine from France and probably closer than sack to the white wines we know today. Cyder can be used in its place.

"My Lord of Carlile's sack-posset," reported by Sir Kenelm Digby:

Boil a pint of cream with a little cinnamon and mace. Beat well two whole eggs and the yolks of two more and stir into a quarter of a pint of sack [cyder] and then add three ounces of sugar with a little grated nutmeg; bring almost to the boil. Pour on the hot cream from some height, but do not stir. Cover with a dish, and when settled sprinkle a little [caster] sugar with a touch of some ambergris and musk on top.

Another of Digby's recipes, in which the cream is curdled with cyder, is for a much more substantial posset, the thickness provided by grain:

Scald half a pound of French barley with boiling water and bruise it generously by folding it up in a cloth and beating against a hard surface. Boil with three pints of milk until the volume is reduced by a half, stirring constantly. Pour in three pints of cream, continuing with the stirring. When it reaches the boil, add sugar to taste. Boil half a pint of sharp cyder or verjuice and white wine mixed, with sugar to correct the acidity, and to this mixture add the cream, milk and barley mixture, straining out the barley through a coarse sieve. Make sure both are hot (but do not boil again), to ensure curdling. Serve with a scattering of sugar and powdered cinnamon.

According to Digby, syllabubs are (as we might expect) but variations on the same principle:

"My Lady Middlesex makes Syllabubs for little Glasses with spouts, thus. Take three pints of Sweet Cream, one of quick white wine (or Rhenish) and a good wine glassful (better the ¼ of a pint) of Sack: mingle with them about three quarters of a pound of fine Sugar in Powder. Beat all these together with a whisk, till all appeareth converted into froth. Then pour it into your little Syllabub-glasses, and let them stand all night. The next day the Curd will be thick and firm above, and the drink clear under it." Digby recommends in addition a little rosemary, lemon peel, or spices to "quicken the taste".

Those who keep their own cows might be tempted by the following related recipe:

Put a pint of sharp cyder in a bowl, and milk the cow into it (perhaps about three pints). Remove the curd and beat it with cream, sack and sugar. Serve with a sprinkling of sugar in a syllabub pot.

Like possets, syllabubs can be made stiffer by whipping up the ingredients with eggs:

"To make a whip syllabub.

Take the whites of two Eggs, and a pint of cream, six spoonsful of Sack, as much sugar as will sweeten it; then take a Birchen rod and whip it; as it riseth with froth, skim it and put it into the syllabub pot; so continue it with whipping and skimming, till your syllabub pot be full" (Digby).

Apple wine

Apple wines might be considered a legitimate topic to be considered here. In fact, the usual home-made apple wine is a solution of alcohol prepared by fermenting white sugar, flavoured with apples, and various recipes can be found in the amateur wine-making literature. The reader of this book might, however, be interested to learn the recipe of the water cider made and used as his "ordinary drink" by William Harvey, the discoverer of the circulation of the blood. It is partly a small cider and partly an apple wine and the method of making it was noted down by Digby, Harvey's contemporary.[8]

Ingredients
1 bushel (eight gallons) pippins
5 lbs brown sugar
1 pint ale yeast

Method
Slice the apples and boil in twelve gallons of water until it is reduced to nine. Filter through Hippocras-bag [muslin], add the sugar and yeast and allow to ferment for 48 hours. Skim off the head of yeast and allow to stand for another two or three days; again skim off froth, bottle and cork.

Drink within two weeks; do not keep beyond six.

Digby's own method of making cider was similar, but instead of adding sugar, he allowed the boiled liquor to stand on fresh apples for three days. This seems to have added taste, and no doubt supplied the yeast that fermented the final pressed juice. He also supplies us with a recipe for apple juice, prepared in a way very similar to Harvey's cider, but bottled directly after filtering through the Hippocras bag, without fermentation.

Cyser and fruit wines

Although the dictionary tells us that "cyser" is simply an obsolete form of "cyder", there is a wine-making tradition that it is cyder strengthened by the addition of honey before fermentation. Honey on its own fermented in water produces mead, and mead flavoured by fruit juices is melomel; in other words apple melomel is the same thing as cyser. The mixture of apple juice and honey is a wise one. Mead, without any additives, is either cloyingly sweet, or with a rather "hard" taste when dry: old recipes invariably either include a large number of herbs to offset the hardness, or are designed to produce a drink to be consumed while still slightly sweet, and undoubtedly the fruitiness of apple juice is precisely what simple mead lacks. Honey was the universal sweetener in the days before sugar became available from the West Indies, and it was extensively used in making fermented drinks, home-produced "wines", in the seventeenth century and earlier.

Just as apple juice supplies what is lacking in honey, so honey can be used to improve cyder left over from blending. It can be used to promote a gentle fermentation in flat cyder, to bring it back into condition, in the way in which it was used by Digby to refresh ale. It can also be used to correct an acid cyder, for immediate drinking. The cyderist who also makes fruit wines will find that an indifferent wine, particularly of a pigmented fruit like damsons or elderberries, will make a very attractive drink when mixed with properly conditioned cyder, very cold. Even commercial bottled ciders are useful.

Indeed, the cyderist may well deliberately embark on the production of fruit wines for their intrinsic attractiveness, as well as for blending purposes. In doing so, he will be following the practice of his seventeenth-century forebears, who made a very wide range of drinks from a number of basic ingredients: honey (or sugar) or malt to supply the greater part of the alcohol; fruit juices to supply the taste and some alcohol (apples and grapes alone supplying any appreciable quantity); herbs and spices for further taste or for medical purposes. Thus *metheglin* is a mead with herbs and is often used medically, and *hippocras* is a spiced mead, and is so called from the practice of infusing the spices in the liquor while contained in a muslin "sleeve of Hippocrates",: that is, a bag that looked like the sleeve of a gown which the medievals imagined was worn by the Father of Medicine.

Cyderists like Worlidge promoted home-made fruit wines for the same reasons as they advocated cyder: to discourage the import of foreign wines, to save the grain used in making ale and beer for baking, and to promote husbandry. Although during the eighteenth century sugar became cheaper and more convenient than honey as the basis of these fruit wines, undoubtedly the traditional recipes are in origin recipes for melomels, fruit-flavoured meads. Cyser, whether regarded as an apple-flavoured mead or as a honey-fortified cyder, is a medieval drink of the same tradition; and some general remarks on the making of melomels will not be amiss here.

Of all the honeys available at present, English is probably the best for mead, as a basis for cyser and other melomels. Most imported honeys, which are generally cheaper, have come from large-scale operations where the bees are fed on a single type of blossom, such as Tasmanian leatherwood, Hungarian lime or acacia and Canadian clover. This leads to predominance of a single taste and a lack of subtlety; in strong-tasting honeys, like Mexican, and Australian amber, the taste is overpowering. Amateur beekeepers in England, on the other hand, find that their bees gather from the large variety of flowers normally available, and the resultant honey is nicely blended and not heavy in flavour. The simplest advice on the use of honey to make melomels is to use it in place of white sugar in recipes for fruit wines. But do not forget that honey has its own taste, and it may be necessary to reduce the amount of fruit used if the result is not to be too rich. It should rarely be necessary to use more than three pounds of honey per gallon, and no more than one pound for cyser, where the apple juice is already rich in sugar. Incidentally, it is interesting to note that when mead was a common drink, it existed in the same varieties of strength and excellence as cyder and beer: we know from medieval Welsh law that the very best mead was that made from honey which emerged of its own accord from the comb, just as the best wines and cyders were made from the juice that came from the ground fruit before any pressure was applied to the press; mead from the *extracted* honey corresponded to the normal cyder, wine pressed from the fruit and to strong ale from fresh malt; while the weakest mead, drunk by the peasants, was made from the water that was used to wash the last of the honey from the combs, just as ciderkin was the watered reworking of the pomace and small beer was from the spent malt similarly treated.

So when Worlidge (in 1676), Digby (1699) and others give us techniques of making fruit and vegetable wines that were already traditional, they are describing what are probably medieval recipes for melomels, metheglins, hydromels (a medieval term, from English and Irish sources of the eleventh to fourteenth centuries, for "mead") and other meads. Thus Digby's "Meath with raisins" (40 gallons of water, 10 gallons of honey, 40 pounds of raisins . . .) is actually a mead known as a *pyment*, the term for a fermented mixture of grape juice and honey (raisins being dried grapes, "blew Raisins of the Sun" as they were known to our seventeenth-century authors).

Of English fruit domesticated by the seventeenth century the cherry was used principally to flavour imported wine[9] although its juice was sometimes used with sugar to make a domestic fruit wine. A wine was also made of currants, apparently the redcurrant being best known; and unlike the meads, which incorporated a lot of honey and were consequently drunk rather sweet, currant wines employed perhaps a pound of sugar per gallon and so much have been very dry when the fermentation was complete. Like the best cyder, these wines were conditioned in bottle by the addition of a small amount of sugar before corking. On the whole it seems likely that these wines were drunk before they had become completely dry.[10] At one extreme, Digby's currant wine had no added sugar and was ready to drink after as little as a week. The addition of sugar was seen principally as a means of extending the life of the wine in a bottle (or cask) by increasing its strength, and Worlidge recommends at least two months in bottle after a month's preparation.

Domestic wines were also made of gooseberries, elderberries and elderflowers, strawberries, blackberries and mulberries, while their juices, together with those of apricots and peaches, were used to flavour imported wines and sometimes domestic cyder.

Herbs and spices

We have already seen that herbs and spices were used not only to alter the taste of cyder, but to give it medical virtues. In the period when English cyder was at its height, these two uses were not separate activities, but were aspects of the same thing, the preparation of a diet. They would be employed normally by the same person, the cook, more or less under the direction of the head of the household. There were a number of reasons for this: in the case of illness, the visiting physician would not bring medicines with him, but would perhaps prescribe actual medicines to be taken, or perhaps indicate only the *kind* to be used. The number of kinds was not in fact large, and most medicines were cooling or drying, or their opposites; others procured purges, vomiting, sweat or urine, while others were said to strengthen some of the natural or vital faculties. In any event it was left to the apothecary or someone close to the household to name, collect or buy the herbs and spices which formed the greater bulk of the physician's pharmaceutical armoury, and it was normally the person in charge of preparing food – from the fashionable ladies Digby was so fond of quoting, down to their cooks – who would also prepare the medicines, selecting as food for the ill those vegetables (the term is interchangeable with herbs in this period) that had the required virtues.

Thus the "receipts" of the medical writers do not differ in kind from the recipes of the authors of cookery books. Digby quotes as readily Francis Glisson's and Francis Bacon's conserve of roses, for primarily medical reasons, as he quotes Sir John Arundel's white mead for its taste. Herbs and spices, and the cyder and mead they were used in, formed a regular diet not only for ill people, but for those whose dispositions were apt to a certain kind of disorder, in order to correct their fundamental complexion or temperament.

Those who are familiar with herbs will be interested in how they were used three hundred years ago in the drinks of the time. Let us briefly look at Digby's collection of receipts: he has just over a hundred ways of making drinks, most of them mead of one sort of another, and collected from England and Europe. In the course of describing them, about 120 herbs and spices are mentioned. All the herbs, he says, with the exception of rosemary, give a "physical", i.e. medical, taste, and we may suppose they were normally used, in metheglins for example, for their medical virtues. "Physical" taste he opposed to "fine", the taste of the spices and lemon peel, components chosen primarily for their taste.

If we look at enough of these recipes we can see which were the most popular of the traditional herbs and spices, and we can thus form a reasonable idea of what the meads and cyders of the time, when made in this way, tasted like. It appears at once that the most popular ingredient of the meads and metheglins described by Digby was ginger, used in 70 per cent of all receipts; cloves were used in more than half, while cinnamon and nutmeg were used in 40 per cent. Mace was slightly less popular (28 per cent). It was very generally agreed then, that spices were very important. The aim was not to give a hot spicy flavour as in a mulled wine, but almost imperceptibly to raise the "life" or "spirits" of the taste, and to this end the spices were hung in a muslin bag – the sleeve of Hippocrates – in the liquor as the fermentation went on. All these spices were reckoned hot and dry in the second and third degrees, and so aided the vital processes, which depended on heat, and counteracted any phlegmatic tendency of the drink, often thought to be found in cyder. Inasmuch as these spices were used because "they are good for you", their popularity reinforces the image the seventeenth-century Englishman had of himself as phlegmatic.

In contrast to the spices, the herbs were normally employed at the early stages of making the drink, being boiled with the honey in the preparation of mead, or added as a decoction. Far and away the most popular herb was rosemary, used in nearly two thirds of all of these receipts; its nearest rival was thyme, used in a little over a third. Rosemary was esteemed greatly in medicine, and Culpeper rated it as high as any other "not only for physical but for civil purposes", that is, for medical and culinary use. Again, it was reckoned a heating agent, useful in correcting the coldness of cyder and of its English drinker. Like so many herbs its virtues were thought to have greater effect on the body when taken with wine, a medical technique which was one end of a spectrum that also included simple flavouring for culinary purposes.

The other more popular herbs were also warming: thyme was anti-phlegmatic, and so good for the lungs, and sweet marjoram (in one third of all recipes) warmed the brain. When we come to examine the herbs lower down on the scale of popularity, we find that "hotness" is no longer a characteristic, and there are a range of herbs from bayleaves (in a quarter of the receipts) to scabious (in one tenth) that are of balanced "temper", neither hot nor cold. Their principal virtues were thought to be in opening or closing the various pores of the body and so securing a variety of evacuations or retentions. Thus agrimony, often taken in wine, was said to be drying and binding, and so useful for wounds. These virtues were associated with the pair of opposite qualities, wet and dry, that balanced the analogous pair, the hot-cold, of the fundamental constitution of the body. A good reason for adding a herb of this range to an English drink was that its qualities encouraged the evacuation or destruction of phlegm, as scabious was wont to do; parsley was one of the "five opening roots", and so encouraged the evacuation of noxious humours. Culpeper welcomed the "old fashioned" habit of cooking fish with fennel on the grounds that the virtue of fennel was to break up and remove the phlegm that was so characteristic of fish. Here the traditions of cooking and medicine are at one: undoubtedly fish tastes better when cooked with fennel, and undoubtedly one of the reasons it continued to be cooked with fennel was because the doctors asserted it was good for you.

Also in this middle range of "temperate" and moderately popular herbs are some whose virtue was cold rather than hot. Although of less use against the prevailing disposition of the English, these herbs had important uses in reducing fevers and inflammations. Borage and bugloss were held to reduce the heat of fevers, and to strengthen the parts; betony, in wine or mead, was used for putrid fevers, and most of this group had other useful virtues.

Below this group in popularity was another – used in rather less than 10 per cent of the recipes – where the predominant virtue was coldness: strawberry and violet in particular, and their leaves, petals and fruits were held to be effective simple cooling medicines.

Cooking with cyder

Cyder will take the place of wine in many recipes. It has more tannin than white wine and has something of the effect of red wine. Below are a number of recipes where cyder has been found particularly appropriate. Some have been modified from those published by the cider firms: the source of these is indicated. Acknowledgement is also made where the recipes have already been published elsewhere.

SOUPS

Crowcombe Chicken Soup
(Taunton)

Ingredients

1 large carrot, grated
1 medium-sized onion, finely chopped
½ green pepper, finely chopped
2 sticks celery, finely chopped
1 oz butter

2¼ pints chicken stock
¾ pint dry cyder
4 oz cooked chicken, finely diced
1½ oz small soup pasta (stars, rings, alphabets)
salt and pepper

Method

Gently fry carrot, onion, green pepper and celery in butter for 4–5 minutes. Add chicken stock and cyder, and bring to the boil. Cover, and simmer very gently for 15–20 minutes. Add chicken, pasta and seasoning, and continue to simmer for 6–10 minutes, or until pasta is cooked.

Makes approximately 3 pints soup.

Pheasant Soup
(Adapted from Robin McDouall, *Cooking with Wine*, Penguin, 1968)

Ingredients

1 dessertspoon butter
2½ pints water
1 pheasant carcase

2 onions
½ pint old cyder
Salt and pepper

Method

The pheasant carcase must have a reasonable amount of meat still on it – the bones alone will not make a very good soup, though they will make adequate stock.

Chop the onions and cook them in butter. Break up the pheasant and add the pieces to the onion. Cover with water. Season. Simmer for several hours, skimming off the fat. Remove the bones. Put the pheasant meat and onion through a mill, strain on the cooking liquor, bring to the boil and skim. Add the cyder (you may need less if it is strongly flavoured) and salt and pepper to taste. If you have a little of the breast of pheasant left over, chop it up and stir it into the soup as a garnish.

MEAT RECIPES

Rabbit and cyder casserole

Ingredients

½ pint cyder with two tea-
    spoons Tewkesbury
    mustard
2 rashers streaky bacon cut
    into strips

1 rabbit in pieces
sea salt, black pepper
2 onions, sliced
2 bayleaves
1 level tablespoon flour

Method

Heat the bacon until there is enough fat to brown the rabbit pieces. Remove the pieces from the pan and add the flour: fry until coloured and then add the cyder to make the sauce. Add rabbit, bayleaves, salt and pepper, onions, cover and simmer for 1 hour or more. Remove rib bones. Garnish with grilled mushrooms, tomatoes and bacon rolls.

Wrapped sausage

Ingredients

¼ pint cider
1 lb pork sausages
1 oz dripping
1 level tablespoon of flour
1 onion
1 small apple

1 teaspoon tomato purée
1 teaspoon Worcester Sauce
2 teaspoons chutney
½ lb packet frozen puff pastry
1 beaten egg

Method

Fry the sausages in the dripping, remove and slice. Chop and fry the onion, mix in flour and cyder to make sauce. Add apple, cored, peeled and sliced, sausage and tomato purée and simmer for 10 minutes. Cool and add Worcester Sauce, chutney, salt and pepper. Roll the pastry into a thin square, put filling into centre and brush edges of pastry with egg. Fold the corners up into the centre and pinch together, leaving small holes at lower corners. Brush pastry with egg and bake for 30 minutes at 425°F (Gas Mark 7) or until well browned.

Old English Pork
(Weston's)

Ingredients

1½ lb lean pork	½ pint stock
1 chopped onion	½ pint cyder
1 oz butter	½ lb peeled, cored and sliced
1½ oz flour	apples

Method

Cut the pork into 1-inch cubes. Melt butter in pan and gently fry the onion and pork for 5 minutes. Stir in the flour and cook for 1 minute. Stir in the stock and cyder. Boil, stirring, for 1 minute. Add seasoning. Cook in a 2½-pint covered dish in a hot oven (375°F, Gas Mark 5), for 1½ hours. Add apples ½ hour before serving. Serve with boiled or jacket potatoes.

Glazed gammon and spiced peaches
(Weston's)

Ingredients

4 lb boned and rolled gammon	FOR THE PEACHES:
1 pint cyder	1 lb tin of peach halves
1 level tablespoon dry mustard	1 oz demerara sugar
4 oz demerara sugar	½ level teaspoon cinnamon
	2 tablespoons peach juice
	4 tablespoons cider vinegar
	mustard and cress

Method

Soak gammon joint overnight before cooking. Put the joint in a large pan and add the cyder and enough water to cover. Bring to the boil and simmer gently, allowing 20 minutes to the pound. Peel off skin when cooked.

Mix together the sugar and the mustard and cover the fat

surface of the joint. Brown this surface by putting in a hot oven (425°F, Gas Mark 7) for 15 minutes. (Cover lean meat with tin foil to avoid drying out.)

Drain the peaches. Dissolve the sugar in the vinegar, peach juice and cinnamon in a large flat pan. Add peach halves, cut side down, and poach gently for 15 minutes. Arrange cress and peaches around bacon. Serve with sweetcorn, peas and creamed potatoes.

Pork with cyder cream sauce
(Taunton)

Ingredients

1¼ lb pork fillet or 8 thin pork steaks	6 oz mushrooms, sliced
2 level teaspoons flour	½ pint cyder
2 oz butter	salt and pepper
1 large onion, finely chopped	4 tablespoons double cream
	chopped parsley

Method

Cut pork fillet into 8 pieces. Place each piece between 2 sheets of greaseproof paper and beat with a meat hammer until ¼ inch thick. Coat pork with some of the flour. Melt butter and fry pork slowly for about 3 minutes on each side. Drain well and keep pork warm. Add onions and mushrooms to pan, and cook slowly until tender but not brown. Stir in remaining flour and cook for 1 minute. Remove from heat and stir in cyder. Stir and cook for 1 minute. Add cooked pork and seasoning, and then stir in cream. Heat through, but do not boil. Garnish with chopped parsley.

Bacon with potato pasty
(Taunton)

Ingredients

3½ lb joint collar bacon	1 onion stuck with 6 cloves
4 carrots	1 pint cyder

Method

Soak bacon for 3–4 hours. Put into large saucepan with carrots

153

and onion. Pour in cyder and bring to boil. Cover and simmer until tender, allowing 20 minutes to the pound plus 20 minutes.

Pasty

8 oz plain flour	1 lb potatoes, peeled and
salt	thinly sliced
2 oz butter	2 oz cheese
2 oz lard	4 tablespoons double cream
	beaten egg for glaze

Method

Sieve flour and salt into basin. Rub in the fat until mixture resembles fine breadcrumbs. Mix to a firm dough with water. Roll out half the pastry and use to line the bottom of a 7–8-inch pie plate. Bring potatoes to boil, drain and place half in pie dish. Season and sprinkle over 1 oz cheese, then follow with rest of potatoes and cheese. Pour the cream over the potatoes. Roll out remaining pastry as lid for pie. Brush with glaze and bake in a moderate oven (350°F, Gas Mark 4), for 1–1¼ hours. Serve with the bacon.

Cyder Ham

Ingredients

dry cyder	6 or 7 peppercorns
brown sugar	uncooked ham

Method

Soak the ham in cyder (commercial cider will do) overnight or preferably longer. Put into a boiling pan with *fresh* cyder to cover it, and the peppercorns. Bring to boil, skim and simmer for 20 minutes per pound of ham. Remove skin and fat from ham and put it into a baking tin, covering the whole of the exposed surface with a stiff paste made from the cyder-ham stock and brown sugar. Place in hottest part of a hot oven until the paste becomes crisp and then remove to a low shelf for a further 20 minutes.

Cyder Brisket

Ingredients

beef brisket, about 2 lb in	1 oz dripping
weight	teaspoon of flour
⅓ pint stock	1 onion

154

bayleaves   ½ pint cyder
salt and pepper

Method
Marinade the beef overnight in the cyder, with the onion, bayleaves and pepper. Melt the dripping in a pan and brown the
beef on each side. Add half the marinade juice, a little salt and a
little fresh cyder, and cook on the lowest heat until tender. Mix
in the stock and flour as a sauce.

FISH RECIPES

Brittany Cod
(*The Times Cookery Book*, Hodder & Stoughton/The Times, 1963)

Ingredients

4 half-pound cod steaks	2 finely chopped carrots
1 pint chicken stock	1 very small finely chopped
¼ pint dry cyder	clove of garlic
2 oz butter	½ lb mushrooms, finely sliced
2 tablespoons flour	1 egg yolk
4 finely chopped shallots	salt and pepper

Method
Melt the butter in a small saucepan, add all the vegetables and
very little salt and pepper, cover tightly and set over lowest possible heat. After the vegetables have been cooking for a half hour,
put the cod into another pan with the stock, cyder, salt and
pepper and cook in the same way as for the Fresh Haddock au
Gratin (see page 157). When it is done, remove from the stock
and keep hot. Whisk the egg. Take out about a cupful of the
stock, let it cool slightly then whisk it into the egg.
   Stir the flour into the vegetables, little by little. When it is
smooth, stir in, slowly, enough of the fish stock to make a fairly
thin sauce. Let this boil for 2 to 3 minutes stirring all the time.
Taste and adjust the seasoning, then take the pan off the stove,
stir in the egg mixture, cover the pan and set it in a baking tin of

hot water over the lowest possible heat – it must not boil – for about 3 minutes and serve poured over the cod.

Cyder fish cakes

Ingredients

1 lb cod or fresh haddock	½ lb potatoes
1 oz butter	breadcrumbs
1 egg	1 pint cyder
chopped parsley	salt and pepper

Method

Gently poach fish in cyder for 15 minutes. Boil and mash potatoes. Drain fish and mix well with other ingredients, cut into square or round shapes, sprinkle with breadcrumbs and bake in a moderate oven until brown (15–20 minutes).

Fillets of sole in cyder
(*Cooking with Wine*)

Ingredients

8 fillets of sole	1 tablespoon butter
¼ bottle cyder	1 dessertspoon flour
salt and pepper	

Method

Butter a fireproof dish and lay in the fillets. Season, cover with cyder. Cook in a moderate oven (350°F, Gas Mark 4) with a piece of greaseproof paper on the top for about 20–30 minutes. Take the fillets out and keep them warm. Reduce the cooking liquor in a saucepan. Correct the seasoning. Add, a small piece at a time, some *beurre manié* – the flour worked into half the butter – to thicken the sauce. Add the rest of the butter in small pieces. Pour this sauce over the fillets and put the dish under a grill for a minute.

Herrings in cyder
(Mary Berry, *Cider for All Seasons*, Woodhead-Faulkner, 1977)

Ingredients

4 herrings	1 small onion, finely chopped
salt and pepper	1 apple, finely chopped

1 tablespoon chopped parsley   ½ pint dry cyder
butter

Method
Remove the bones from the herrings, clean and lay flat. Season
the inside of the fish with salt and pepper. Mix the onion, apple
and parsley together and spread over the herrings. Roll up.
Butter an ovenproof dish and lay the fish in it. Pour the cyder
around them and bake in the oven (350°F, Gas Mark 4) for about
40 minutes. Serve the herrings with cyder spooned over them.

Fresh Haddock au Gratin
(modified from *The Times Cookery Book*)

Ingredients

2–2½ lb haddock	½ pint very thick Béchamel
1 bouquet garni	sauce made with about half
¼ pint cyder vinegar	the usual quantity of milk
¾ lb tomatoes	2 rashers streaky bacon
salt, pepper and 3–4 pepper-	water
corns	

Method
Put the fish into a pan with the bouquet garni, vinegar, 1 pint of
water, a very little salt and the peppercorns. Bring slowly to the
boil, skimming as the scum rises, then poach until the flesh is
just beginning to come away from the bone. Lift the fish out carefully, remove the skin and put the haddock into a greased ovenproof dish.

Boil up the fish stock and reduce it until there is about ½ pint
left. Cut the bacon into very small dice, and fry for 1 minute.

When the fish stock has reduced, strain it then stir it little by
little into the Béchamel over low heat until the sauce is the right
consistency. Stir in the bacon, simmer for a minute or so, then
taste and adjust the seasoning. Cut the tomatoes in half and set
them round the haddock, cut side up and dusted with a little salt
and pepper. Pour the sauce over the fish and tomatoes and dot
with the butter. Bake in a moderate oven (350°F, Gas Mark 4) for

20 minutes, and then in a fairly hot oven (425°F, Gas Mark 7), until the sauce bubbles and begins to colour.

Minehead Mackerel
(Taunton)

Ingredients

¾ oz butter

¾ oz plain flour

½ pint cyder

3 oz Cheddar cheese, grated

1 eating apple, peeled, cored
   and grated

salt and pepper

Method

Melt the butter in a saucepan, add flour and cook for a minute. Remove from heat and gradually stir in cyder. Return to the heat, bring to the boil, stirring. Remove from heat, add grated cheese and stir until melted. Add apple and seasoning, mix well, and heat through. Serve hot with grilled mackerel or herrings.
   Serves 4.

Blue Anchor Pie
(Taunton)

Ingredients

14 oz packet frozen puff pastry

2 oz butter

2 oz plain flour

¾ pint cyder

½ pint of milk

1½ lb haddock fillet, gently
   poached

4 eggs, hard-boiled

½ lb tomatoes

salt and pepper

Method

Melt butter in a pan, add flour, and cook for a minute. Remove from heat, and gradually stir in the cyder and milk. Return to heat and bring to the boil, stirring. Cook for a minute, remove from heat. Flake haddock, and chop eggs and tomatoes. Add haddock, eggs, tomatoes and seasoning to sauce. Pour mixture into a 3-pint pie dish. Place a funnel in the centre of the dish. Roll out the pastry and place over the pie dish. Decorate with a pastry "flower" if liked. Bake in a hot oven (425°F, Gas Mark 7) for 20–25 minutes.
Serves 4–6.

Dunster Plaice
(Taunton)

Ingredients

12 oz packet frozen plaice
fillets, thawed
salt and pepper
1 pint cyder
1 oz gelatine
1 tomato (cut into 8 wedges)

8 oz cottage cheese, sieved
2–3 oz cucumber, peeled and
diced
1 medium-sized stick celery,
chopped
1 teaspoon Worcester Sauce
garnish: cucumber slices

Method

Remove skin from plaice fillets, cut each in half lengthways and season with salt and pepper. Roll up plaice fillets from the narrow end and place in a saucepan or frying pan. Add ½ pint of the cyder, bring to the boil, cover and poach gently for 5 minutes. Drain well, reserving liquid, and leave until plaice is completely cold. Put ½ oz of gelatine and 3 tablespoons of the remaining cyder (not the cooking liquor) into a small basin, and dissolve over a pan of hot water. Stir in remaining cyder. Pour a little of this mixture into a 7-inch round cake tin, just to cover the base. Leave in a cool place until set. Arrange plaice and tomato in the set cyder jelly, and pour on remaining gelatine mixture. Leave in a cool place until set. Dissolve remaining ½ oz gelatine in a little of the reserved cooking liquor (in a basin over a pan of hot water.) Stir in remaining cooking liquor. Mix together cottage cheese and cucumber, celery and Worcester Sauce, and gradually add cooking liquor and gelatine mixture. Mix well. Pour on to set cyder and plaice, making sure that plaice is completely covered. Allow to set in a cool place. To turn out, dip cake tin into hot water, and turn on to a serving plate. Garnish with slices of cucumber.

Serves 4–6.

Moules Marinières
(*Cider for All Seasons*)

When buying mussels allow 1½ pints per person. Take care not to overcook them – they take only a few minutes, just until the shells open.

Ingredients

6 pints fresh mussels	freshly ground black pepper
1 oz butter	½ pint dry cyder
4 shallots	salt
4 parsley stalks	chopped parsley
2 sprigs fresh thyme or ¼ level teaspoon dried thyme	For the *beurre manié:*
	1 oz soft butter
1 bayleaf	½ oz flour

Method

Scrape and clean each mussel with a strong knife, removing every trace of seaweed, mud and beard. Wash in several changes of water, discarding any badly chipped or cracked ones that do not close tightly. Mussels which remain open are dead and should not be used. Drain the mussels in a colander. Melt the butter in a large pan over a low heat. Peel and chop the shallots, add to the pan and fry until they are soft but not brown. Add herbs, pepper, cyder and mussels to the pan, cover with a tight-fitting lid and cook quickly, shaking the pan constantly until the mussels are open (about 5 to 6 minutes). Lift the mussels out, discard the empty half of the shell and keep hot in a covered dish. Reduce the liquor to about ½ pint. Remove the fresh thyme, parsley stalks and bayleaf.

Blend the flour and butter for the *beurre manié* to a smooth paste. Drop the *beurre manié* into the simmering stock a teaspoon at a time and whisk it until the stock is smooth and has thickened. Add more pepper and salt if necessary. Pour the stock over the mussels and scatter with plenty of chopped parsley.

Serve with French bread and butter.

POULTRY AND GAME RECIPES

Quantock Chicken
(Taunton)

Ingredients

one (3 lb) chicken, jointed	just under ½ pint cyder
1 green pepper, de-seeded and chopped	salt and pepper
	5 oz carton natural yoghurt
4 oz mushrooms, – halved	1 tablespoon chopped parsley
1 onion, chopped	

Method
Put chicken, green pepper, mushrooms, onion, cyder and seasoning into an ovenproof casserole dish. Cover, and cook in a moderate oven (Gas Mark 4, 350°F) for about 1½ hours. Remove lid, pour over yoghurt, sprinkle with chopped parsley and serve.

Serves 4–5.

Poacher's Pigeon Casserole
(Cider for All Seasons)
(Other game such as pheasant and grouse may be cooked in this way)

Ingredients

4 pigeons	orange
3 tablespoons oil	1 tablespoon redcurrant jelly
½ peeled button onions	½ lb chestnuts, peeled and
1 rounded tablespoon flour	skinned
¾ pint dry cyder	salt and pepper
grated rind and juice of half an	chopped parsley

Method
Heat the oven to 350°F (180°C) Gas Mark 4.

Cut each pigeon in half along the breastbone and trim off the backbone and wings to leave just the breast and thick part of the leg.

Heat the oil in a large pan and fry the pigeons and onions in the oil for 3 to 4 minutes until brown. Transfer to a large 4½-pint casserole. Stir the flour into the oil remaining in the pan and cook for 1 minute. Add the cyder, orange rind and juice and red currant jelly, and bring to the boil, stirring. Simmer for 2 minutes to thicken and pour over the pigeons. Add the chestnuts and seasoning to the casserole. Cover and cook in the oven until the pigeons are tender (about 1 hour but this can vary with the age of the pigeon).

Serve sprinkled with chopped parsley.

Tarragon Chicken
(Cider for All Seasons)
For special occasions add 2 tablespoons of cream to the sauce just

before serving. Serve with boiled rice.

Ingredients

1 pint packet chicken or celery soup	½ pint dry cyder
1 onion, finely grated	4 chicken joints
1 tablespoon freshly choppped tarragon	freshly ground black pepper

Method

Heat the oven to 350°F (180°C), Gas Mark 4. Mix the packet of soup, onion, tarragon and cyder together in a casserole and drop in the chicken joints. Season with black pepper and bake covered in the oven for 45 minutes or until the chicken is tender. Check seasoning before serving.

Canard au cidre-royal

The distilled cyder that Haines used in the late seventeenth century to make his cyder-royal was essentially the calvados that is still made in France. The finished Cyder-royal was a mixture of such calvados and fresh cyder; here is a recipe that also involves calvados, cyder, and apples for good measure.

Ingredients

STUFFING	4-lb oven-ready duck
3 oz sultanas	GARNISH: Watercress
¼ pint cyder	GLAZE
4 oz fresh white breadcrumbs	4 oz granulated sugar
1 medium-sized onion, peeled and grated	½ pint cyder
1 tablespoon marjoram	1 tablespoon vinegar
2 oz blanched almonds, finely chopped	4 teaspoons cornflour
1 egg, beaten	2 tablespoons calvados
salt	3 small eating apples, peeled, cored, sliced and kept in lemon juice
pepper	¼ pint cyder

Method

Simmer sultanas in cyder for about 20 minutes, until all the cyder has been absorbed. Mix breadcrumbs, onion, marjoram, almonds, sultanas, egg and seasoning together. Use to stuff duck. Roast in oven at 400°F (Gas Mark 6) for about 1½ hours, basting occasionally.

Place sugar in a saucepan. Stir continuously over a moderate heat until sugar has dissolved and turned a caramel colour. Remove from heat at once, cool slightly, then add 2 tablespoons cyder and vinegar. (Take care as the addition of the liquid will cause the hot mixture to boil up.) Return to heat and stir to dissolve the caramel. Stir in remaining cyder. Blend cornflour with calvados, and stir into the caramel mixture. Bring to boil, stirring. Simmer for 5 minutes.

Poach apple rings in cider until tender. Serve duck with glaze poured over, then surround with apple slices, and garnish with watercress. (4 servings)

When using an 8-lb goose, simply double the recipe for the stuffing and glaze.

PUDDINGS, ETC.

Yeovil Baked Pears
(Taunton)

Ingredients

2 oz sultanas
¼ pint sweet cyder
4 firm pears (cored, skinned and halved)

½–1 oz demerara sugar
½ oz butter

Method

Put sultanas and cyder into a small saucepan. Bring to the boil. Remove from the heat and allow to stand for 15 minutes. Put pears in a shallow ovenproof dish. Pour cyder and sultanas over pears. Sprinkle with sugar and dot with butter. Cover and cook in a moderate oven (350°F, Gas Mark 4) for about 35 minutes. Serve with double cream.

Serves 4.

Brendon Hills Pancakes
(Taunton)

Ingredients

Cyder Butter:

4 oz plain flour (sieved)

½ oz caster sugar
1 large egg
½ pint dry cyder
To cook:- lard or cooking fat

Sauce: 8 oz can peaches
8 oz can pears
¼ pint sweet cyder
1 level tablespoon arrowroot
1 tablespoon lemon juice

Method

Put flour and caster sugar into a basin. Make a well in the centre and add egg and half the dry cyder. Beat well until smooth. Gradually add remaining dry cyder beating well. Use batter to make 8 pancakes in the usual way. To make sauce, drain peaches and pears, reserving syrup from cans. Chop fruit. Bring ¼ pint of syrup and the sweet cyder to the boil in a saucepan. Mix arrowroot with lemon juice until smooth, and pour on cyder mixture. Return to the pan, bring to the boil, stirring, and cook for a minute. Add pears and peaches, and heat through. To serve, fold each pancake into four, and pour sauce over pancakes. Serve hot.

Serves 4.

A First-Rate Plum Pudding

(*Cider for All Seasons*)

Ingredients

8 oz self-raising flour
1 level teaspoon mixed spice
½ level teaspoon grated
   nutmeg
1 level teaspoon salt
12 oz currants
12 oz sultanas
12 oz stoned raisins
12 oz fresh white breadcrumbs
12 oz suet, finely chopped

4 oz candied peel, finely
   chopped
2 oz almonds, blanched and
   chopped
1 cooking apple, peeled, cored
   and grated
grated rind and juice of 1
   orange
1 lb soft brown sugar
6 eggs, beaten
¼ pint extra-dry cyder

Method

Grease two 2½-pint pudding basins.

Sift together the flour, mixed spice, nutmeg and salt.

Put the dried fruit into a bowl with the breadcrumbs, suet, peel, almonds, grated apple, orange rind and juice. Stir in the spiced flour and sugar. Finally add the eggs and cyder. Stir the mixture well, then turn into the basins. Cover the tops with greaseproof paper and a foil lid and let the puddings simmer gently in a pan for about 7 hours. Lift them out of the pan, leaving the foil and greaseproof paper in place. Cool and store the puddings.

This old-fashioned rich Christmas pudding improves with keeping.

Simmer for a further 3 hours before serving.

Mincemeat
(Cider for All Seasons)

Ingredients

1½ lb stoned raisins	6 oz shredded suet
½ lb cooking apples	½ level teaspoon mixed spice
4 oz candied peel	2 lemons
12 oz currants	1 lb soft brown sugar
8 oz sultanas	6 tablespoons extra dry cyder

Method

Finely chop or mince the raisins and peel. Peel, core and mince or chop the apples. Place in a large bowl with the other fruit, suet and spice. Grate the rind and squeeze the juice from the lemons. Add to the fruit with the sugar and cyder. Mix well.

Cover the bowl and leave to stand overnight. Next day turn into clean jars, cover and label.

Caramelized Bananas
(Cider for All Seasons)

Ingredients

8 bananas	¼ pineapple juice
2 oz butter	2 oz demerara sugar

Method

Peel and slice the bananas. Melt the butter in a large frying pan and fry the bananas until slightly coloured. Add the apple juice and sugar and boil rapidly until thick and treacly.

Serve at once with cream.

Cooking with apples

In a "hit" year, the cyderist may well have more apples on his hands than he knows what to do with, and may welcome ways of using them in cooking. This is not the place to give a list of recipes in the fashion of a modern cookery book, but as a starting point, the cyderist might like to consider some methods used three hundred years ago, by Sir Kenelm Digby. (Not all cyder fruit is suitable for cooking: avoid the more astringent varieties and choose the blander, like Kingston Black, or Tom Putt.)

APPLES IN GELLY

My Lady Paget makes her fine preserved Pippins, thus: They are done best, when Pippins are in their prime for quickness, which is in November. Make your Pippin-water as strong as you can of the Apples, and that it may be the less boiled, and consequently the paler, put in at first the greatest quantity of pared and quartered Apples, the water will bear. To every Pint of Pippin-water add (when you put the Sugar to it) a quarter of a pint of fair spring-water, that will bear soap (of which sort only you must use) and use half a pound of Sugar, the purest double refined. If you will have much gelly, two pippins finely pared and whole, will be enough; you may put in more, if you will have a greater proportion of substance to the gelly. Put at first but half the Sugar to the Liquor; for so it will be the paler. Boil the Apples by themselves in fair water, with a very little Sugar, to make them tender; then put them into the liquor, and the rest, the other half of the Sugar with them. Boil them with a quick fire, till they be enough, and the liquor do gelly, and that you see the Apples look very clear, and as though they were transparent. You must put the juyce of two Limons and half an Orange to this in the due time. Every Pippin should be lapped over in a broad-pill of Orange; which you must prepare thus. Pare your Orange broad and very thin, and all hanging together, rub it with Salt, prick it and boil it in several waters, to take away the bitterness, and make it tender. Then preserve it by it self with sufficient quantity of Sugar. When it is thoroughly done, and very tender (which you must cast to do before hand, to be ready when the Apples are ready to be put up) take them out of their Syrup, and lap every Pippin in an Orange-peel, and put them into a pot or glass and pour the liquor upon them: which will be gelly over and About the Apples, when all is cold. This proportion of liquor, Apples, and Orange-peels, will take up about three quarters of a pound of Sugar in all. If you would keep them any time, you must put in weight for weight of Sugar.

I conceive Apple-John's instead of Pippins will do better, both for the Gelly and Syrup; especially at the latter end of the year; and I like them thin sliced, rather than whole: and the Orange-peels scattered among them in little pieces or chipps.

SYRUP OF PIPPINS

Quarter and Core your Pippins; then stamp them in a Mortar, and strain out the Juyce. Let it settle, that the thick dregs may go to the bottom; then pour off the clear; and to have it more clear and pure, filter it through sucking Paper in a glass funnel. To one pound of this take one pound and a half of pure double refined Sugar, and boil it very gently (scarce simpringly, and but a very little while) till you have scummed away all the froth and foulness (which will be but little) and that it be the consistence of Syrup. If you put two pound of Sugar to one pound of juyce, you must boil it more & stronglier. This will keep longer but the colour is not so fine. It is of a deeper yellow. If you put but equal parts of juyce and Sugar, you must not boil it, but set it in a *Cucurbite in bulliente Balneo* [i.e. in a vessel itself heated by boiling water] till all the scum be taken away, and the Sugar well dissolved. This will be very pale and pleasant, but will not keep long.

You may make your Syrup with a strong decoction of Apples in water (as when you make gelly of Pippins) when they are green; but when they are old and mellow, the substance of the Apple will dissolve into pap, by boiling in water.

Take three or four spoonfuls of this Syrup in a large draught of fountain water, or small posset-Ale, *pro ardore urinæ*, to cool and smoothen, 2 or 3 times day.

GELLY OF PIPPINS OR JOHN-APPLES

Cut your Apples into quarters (either pared or unpared). Boil them in a sufficient quantity of water, till it be very strong of the Apples. Take the clear liquor, and put to it sufficient Sugar to make gelly, and the slices of Apple; so boil them all together, till the slices be enough, and the liquor gelly; or you may boil the slices, in Apple-liquor without Sugar, and make gelly of other liquor, and put the slices into it, when it is gelly, and they be sufficiently boiled. Either way, you must put at the last some juyce of Limon to it; and Amber and Musk if you will. You may do it with halves or quartered Apples, in deep glasses, with store of gelly about them. To have these clear, take the pieces out of the gelly they are boiled in, with a slice so as you may have all the rags run from them, and then put neat clean pieces into clear gelly.

PRESERVED WARDENS

Pare and Core the Wardens, and put a little of the thin rind of a Limon into the hole that the Core leaveth. To every pound of Wardens, take half a pound of Sugar, and half a pint of water. Make a Syrup of your Sugar and Water; when it is well scummed, put it into a Pewter dish, and your Wardens into the Syrup, and cover it with another Pewter dish; and so let this boil very gently, or rather stew, keeping it very well covered, that the steam get out as little as may be. Continue this, till the Wardens are very tender, and very red, which may be in five, or six, or seven hours. Then boil them up to the height the Syrup ought to be kept: which yet will not be well above three or four months. The whole secret of making them red, consisteth in doing them in Pewter, which spoileth other preserves, and in any other mettal these will not be red. If you will have any Amber in them, you may to ten or twelve pounds of Wardens, put in about twenty grains of Amber, and one, or at most, two grains of Musk, ground with a little Sugar, and so put in at the last. Though the Wardens be not covered over with the Syrup in the stewing by a good deal, yet the steam, that riseth and cannot get out, but circulateth, will serve both to stew them, and to make them red and tender.

SWEET MEAT OF APPLES

My Lady Barclay makes her fine Apply-gelly with slices of John apples. Sometimes she mingles a few Pippins with the John's to make the Gelly. But she liketh best the John's single, and the colour is paler. You first fill the glass with slices round-wise cut, and then the Gelly is poured in to fill up the cavities. The Gelly must be boiled to a good stiffness. Then when it is ready to take from the fire, you put in some juyce of Limon, and of Orange too, if you like it: but these must not boil; yet it must stand a while upon the fire stewing in good heat, to have the juyces Incorporate and Penetrate well. You must also put in some Ambergreece, which doth exceeding well in this sweet-meat.

TO STEW WARDENS OR PEARS

Pare them, put them into a Pipkin, with so much Red or Claret Wine and water, *ana*, as will near reach to the top of the Pears. Stew or boil gently, till they grow tender, which may be in two hours. After a while, put in some sticks of Cinnamon bruised and a few Cloves. When they are almost done, put in Sugar enough to season them well and their Syrup, which you pour out upon them in a deep Plate.

TO STEW APPLES

Pare them and cut them into slices. Stew them with Wine and Water as the Pears, and season them in like manner with Spice. Towards the end sweeten them with Sugar, breaking the Apples into Pap by stirring them. When you are ready to take them off, put in good store of fresh-butter, and incorporate it well with them, by stirring them together. You stew these between two dishes. The quickest Apples are the best.

(From *The Closet of Sir Kenelm Digby Knight Opened*)

Folklore

Apart from the different ways of consuming cider, the drink also had a *ritual* use in the past. The practices associated with folklore are probably very much older than the cider used in them; common cider probably entered the ritual practices of common folk in the seventeenth century. Any vestige of a relationship between the survival of the Celts in the West Country, mistletoe, apples and cider, has long been lost.

Nineteenth-century Herefordshire labourers poured a little cider on the ground when drinking. They told an interested folk-lorist that this was a "donation" to the gods; perhaps they meant "libation" and perhaps they were pulling her leg.[11] Generally, the ritual habits in which cider was involved were governed by the agricultural year. Anyone found working on New Year's Day was "captured", placed on a ladder and taken round to the farm-house, where the company claimed cider from the farmer. Another custom connected with New Year, and kept up until the end of the nineteenth century, was "burning the bush". The bush was a globe of hawthorn, hung up in the kitchen through-out the year, like mistletoe. The ceremony often began on New Year's Eve, when the labourers liked to drink more cider than usual – which they called "burying Old Tom" –probably without break until, early in the morning, the bush was carried out to the earliest sown wheatfield and burnt on a large fire of straw and bushes. While it was burning the new one was made, scorching the ends of the twigs in the fire of the old. At Shobdon at least, they poured cider over the embers after the new bush had been made. While the cider may be a recent addition to an ancient ritual, the pouring itself, another "donation" or libation to the gods, is probably a very much older act. At Birley Court, they made two bushes, one for the Master and one for the eldest child. Parts of the burning "bush" were carried over twelve ridges of the old field system by one of the men, who dropped a fragment on to each ridge. At Brinsop, the carrying of the pyre over the ridges was said to destroy evil spirits between midnight on New Year's Eve and six o'clock in the next morning. It was a bad omen for the next year's crops if the fire went out before the twelfth ridge was reached. An alternative tradition was to light twelve bundles of hay from each other, the first being lit from the bush and the twelve being carried over the ridges.

> Then the men stand in a ring round the fire and "holloa auld cider". They sing on one very deep note, very slowly, holding each syllable as long as possible, "Auld-Ci-der". The "der" becomes a sort of growl at the end, and is an octave below the first two notes; it has a weird dirge-like effect. This is repeated thrice, bowing as low as possible as each note is sung, nine bows altogether. Then follows cheering and drinking, cider and cake being provided for the purpose.[12]

At Hill Court, Ross, they sang instead (in 1860): "Auld cider for ever, as plenty as water." "Old cider" became a popular phrase, and formed a joyful refrain to a song written on the repeal of the eighteenth-century cider tax:

> Likewise to Pitt and Dowdeswell, we'll stretch our throats still
> wider
> And all the Moccas hills shall echo back –
> OLD CIDER!

It may well be that the "auld cider" ceremony, as Leather says, was purificatory and fertilizing. Another custom in which the use of cider seems to have been a comparatively recent addition (that is, no more than three centuries old) was the celebration of Twelfth Night. In the evening before Twelfth Day, the master of the house went out to a field where wheat was growing, and twelve small fires and one large were lit in the dusk. Toasts were drunk in old cider to those present around the largest fire, on high ground, and the subsequent cheer and hallooing was answered from neighbouring fields and villages. British camps at the summits of such hills as Dinedor were popular locations for these fires. Following these toasts, a cake baked with a hole in the middle was placed around the horn of one of the cattle and a traditional supplication made for the next year's crop. The animal was made to toss the cake, either by a goad or by throwing cider at it, and prognostications were made as to the future of the crops or of the cake, depending on its landing behind or before.

Another eighteenth-century ritual of Twelfth Night (that is, old Christmas Day) was that, on the eve of Twelfth Day, the farmer and his men carried a large pitcher of cider into the orchard and, standing round a tree, shouted three times:

Here's to thee old apple tree
Whence thou mayst bud and whence thou mayst blow!
And whence thou mayst bear apples enow:

Hats full, caps full,
Bushel, bushel, sacks full,
And my pockets full too.
Huzzah, huzzah

A similar verse was recited in Somerset until the late nineteenth century.

The cake that often played a part in these ceremonies was generally plum cake, and plum cake and old cider were frequent companions in old Herefordshire customs. In the corn-showing on Easter Day, kept up until the very end of the last century in Dilwyn and Henwood, the bailiff, the workers and their families went on to the wheatfield and, joining hands, recited a verse as they marched across the field, asking God for a good harvest for the master. At Lulham, in the parish of Madley, and at St Margarets, a small piece of the cake was buried, and cider from the wooden costrels was poured over it. Perhaps even earlier cake and cider were buried in orchards in a very natural ceremony to encourage fruitfulness the following year; it was certainly performed in the middle of the nineteenth century in Dorstone and Peterchurch. Cake and cider also figured in the Easter ritual of picking the cockle out of the corn, and in the Broomy Hill May Day, at Hereford, cake and cider were consumed at the Maypole dances at the end of the eighteenth century.

As the year progressed, from New Year through Easter to the summer, other customs were practised in the cider counties. Aubrey in the seventeenth century described a midsummer eve custom of lighting fires in the fields of Herefordshire to bless the apples. He noted the same thing in Somerset in 1635, although the purpose was not clearly stated. In north Herefordshire it was held that the orchards had to be blessed on St Peter's Day, shortly after midsummer, or the crop would fail. This was recorded at Elton in 1880 and it was additionally remarked that a shower of rain upon the people in the orchard blessing it was a good omen. In current mythology apples are more closely connected with St Swithin, and are said to be uneatable until his day, 15th July. It is also commonly said that if it rains on St Swithin's Day it will rain for forty days after. There may be some connection between the blessing of the apples and rain, which was perhaps seen as a sign of fertility:

But when the blackning clouds in sprinkling showr's
Distil, from the high summits down the rain
The rain runs trickling; with the fertile moisture cheer'd
The orchats smile; joyous the farmers see
Their thriving plants, and bless the heavenly dew.

It is difficult to imagine what apples became eatable even shortly after St Swithin's Day, and it would certainly be months later that any cider fruit was fit for use. But the blessing of the trees remained the important thing. In Eardisland they poured a glass of cider over the trunk of each tree, tapped it three times and blessed it.

Getting in the harvest was naturally a time of celebration and great consumption of cider. The last small cluster of corn to be cut was tied together in a particular way and the workmen threw their sickles at it from a distance to cut it down, sometimes with their backs to it. This last sheaf, called the "mare", once cut, was carefully plaited up like the "bush" and the mistletoe, and hung in the kitchen throughout the year. After the cutting of the mare, the ceremony of "hallooing auld cider" was performed in the harvest field as in the bush-burning custom, and the company returned to the harvest supper. A "wassail" cup was sometimes used at supper, from which each of those present would take a draught of gin and cider after singing a song, asking a riddle or giving a toast. The wassail bowl at Christmas too contained a punch made of hot cider, gin, nutmeg and sugar.

At the end of life, as at the end of the year, cake and cider again made their appearance. These refreshments were made available even at poor people's funerals. A curious custom at funerals involving food and drink was that of the "sin eater", who for a fee would eat bread and drink ale from a bowl in the room where the corpse was lying, thereby to take upon himself the sins of the deceased, and so "freed him or her from walking after they were dead".

Traditional customs find their place in, and indeed transmute themselves into, traditional tales or legends. One such story concerns a beggar who sought alms from a Herefordshire hamlet. He was turned away from the first cottage empty-handed by the mistress of the house. At the second he was invited in to share the last three apples surviving from the crop of the foregoing autumn. In gratitude he left the mistress of the second house with the mysterious advice to perform the action involved in this act of generosity once more at sunset. She accordingly picked up the last surviving apple at the appointed time, and having placed it upon the shelf turned in surprise to find another in its place. This in turn was removed, to be magically replaced once more. This went on for the hour that separated sunset from the rising of the moon, and replaced much of the treasured apple crop. The news of this happy event soon reached the first housewife, who swore silently to herself that should the beggar call again, she would present him with a gift of money, and at sunset pour money from a bowl. The beggar came; he was duly presented with money and regaled with cider and plum cake; he made a similar promise and left; but alas! in her anxiety to upturn the bowl at sunset, the housewife upset instead the jug of cider, which continued to run over the kitchen floor until moonrise.

174

By way of a glossary

The seventeenth- and eighteenth-century discussion on cyder is a forgotten literature. Some of it survives in an oral tradition among the very few people who make farmhouse and cottage cider today; and to understand properly what was and is said we must know some of the peculiarities of the language of the cyderists.

Two things have contributed to the peculiarity of this language. First the making of cyder was much influenced by its French model, and many of its technical terms are French in origin. We can recall Lord Scudamore as a transmitter of such influence, and again in the nineteenth century the Woolhope Club strove to rejuvenate cyder making by bringing new varieties of fruit from Normandy. (The term "Norman" appended to so many modern varieties reflects this influence, although many such varieties are in fact domestic in origin.) Second, the language of the Herefordshire countryman is far from being standard English. The ways in which his speech differs from that of the politically dominant South-east began to emerge in the two centuries or so which it took for the Saxons to advance against the British from east to west. The difference was felt in the early place names, for example the eastern termination "-worthy" and its relatives (for example Worthing) is regularly "-wardine" in the West: Lugwardine, Bredwardine and many others. The Herefordian's grammar is also different; to give only one example, "her" replaces "she" or "it" as the subject of the sentence. The usage is common and is recorded, for example, by Haggard:[13] a man who had spent all day cleaning out the gubban-hole (cesspit) observed, "That ent a very clean job, mind. When I started her smelt smartish but when I finished – by God! her stank roaring."

Never heavily industrialized, Herefordshire has escaped many of the influences that have turned other English counties into a diffuse suburb. No more traditional a figure can be imagined than the cottage cyderist, using the language of his ancestors as he goes about his business. His first task is to harvest the apples in his orchat by shaking what he can off the

A traditional sight in the 1920s in Herefordshire: a horse harnessed to a mill

trees and pothering off the remainder with a panking-pole some 15 feet long (sometimes hooked and called a "lugg" or "hook pole"). Nowadays he gives little attention to varieties, gathering up the table-fruit – pot-fruit, crinks – together with his cider fruit and storing them in tumps. ("Tump" for "mound" occurs most characteristically in the phrase "unt-tump" for "mole hill".) A good year for apples is known as a hit.

Maturing in the tump, the fruit becomes daddicky, dotey or mosey: that is, from over-ripe to rotten (pears are "beethy"), but approved of for cider. Come Christmas, the fruit is taken into the cider house and put, a bushel or so at a time, on to the central pier of the mill. As the horse pushes the runner around the chase, the cyderist follows, "rowing down" the fruit into the chase with his rowing stick or tammus. To every bushel of apples a bucket or two of water is thrown into the chase for the sup-posed benefit of the end product and to prevent the runner from tushing: that is, sliding around the chase without revolving. A tushing runner would soon collect up the milled fruit (murc, musk, pummice or pomey) so that it would spill over the edge of the chase. To help prevent this, and to allow the mill to grind as much as possible at a grist, the mill is fitted with a kerbing-board, timber of triangular section, sitting on the outer edge of the chase and held in place with iron cramps. To prevent spillage and to prevent any of the fruit from remaining uncrushed, the cyderist scrapes the sides of the chase with his tammus or special musking-board as he follows the horse.

The pummice is removed from the chase with the musking board, or a scoop, and transferred to the press, where it is placed on a hair cloth laid out on the chuter. The hair is folded over the pummice and another laid on top to hold more pummice. Up to a dozen hairs laid in this way make up a cheese, sometimes with the aid of a square frame and moveable battens (or batons). The juice, emerging under the pressure of the screws, leaves the spout of the wooden or stone chuter and collects in a cooler, which can also be made of wood or stone. The last drop of juice to emerge from the pummice when the screws are hard down is very clear, and is tempting to taste; but it is to be drunk with caution, for it is a stronger purgative than the finished cyder. Much more so if it is perry rather than cyder that is being made, and it is said of perry that "it goes round and round like thunder and out like lightning". Haggard reports a cautionary tale about the effects of perry, told to him in 1942 by the son of the squire in question:

The traditional cider-maker keeps his mill in good order. In particular the wooden parts are liable to decay and have to be replaced. This mill has a kerbing-board around the outside edge of the chase, held up by T-shaped iron cramps. Two of the iron cramps, inset in lead, that hold together the stones of the mill are also visible. When the mill has a kerbing-board, the central pier is also sometimes raised to the same height, by a wooden disc, on which the apples are put into a tump, to be rowed down into the chase. Just visible are the shoulder and arm of the ciderist, following his horse as he rows down the fruit. The horse wears blinkers to prevent giddiness

In the 1870s or '80s the Squire introduced his bride to Mr and Mrs Smith at the Home Farm. Mr Smith was suffering from gout and was chair-ridden. Mrs Smith, all of a twitter at the unexpected visit, after fussing round, said: "Now, Ma'am, would you like a glass of sherry, Ma'am, or a glass of perry, Ma'am?" Mrs Squire, who did not like sherry, but had never tasted perry, said she would like a little perry; whereupon from the depths of his chair Mr Smith rumbled: "I should

Ancient wooden-screw press in Herefordshire

have sherry if I was you, Mum, that perry do make you blow terrible and it be werry quick."

The juice is carried from the cooler in a gaun and discharged into the hogshead through a tundish (sometimes "tunpail") both being vessels cut down from small barrels. The rack on which the hogsheads stand is known as a tram, and is designed to prevent the vessels rolling. The beginning of fermentation is indicated when the juice begins to fret – to hiss or sing a little in the vessel; in Devon "fretting" was, traditionally, *excessive* fermentation,

Sharp cider, or that which has gone sour, is known in Herefordshire as "squeal pig", of which it is said that "you need someone to hold you while you drink it". The description refers to the constriction the drinker feels in his throat, and is not a suggestion that pigs would squeal if made to drink the cider. Pigs are said to have refused to eat the famous and astringent Barland perry pear, but the pig in this photograph (probably of the 1920s) seems to be enjoying fragments of crushed apple. It is often said that pigs, allowed to eat discarded pummice that had since fermented, would become tipsy, or "peart". The photograph shows also the portable equipment of the travelling cider-maker: a horse-driven scratter and a mobile twin-screw press

leading to the danger of acetification. The finished cider is known as scrump, scrumpy, or jake: or belly-vengeance.[14] The labourer's costrel, taking with him a gallon or half a gallon of cider into the fields, he called his bottle; consuming his cider immoderately, he became tosticated, peart, or, spending too long in the pub on market-day, market-peart.

Related of a Parish Meeting in Weobley on Wednesday (Hereford market-day). Mr Jones, market peart, attended.

The Clerk: I think it should be a permanent job, gentlemen, but I don't think Mr Jones quite knows the difference between temporary and permanent.

Mr Jones: Oh, don't I – be blowed! I'm drunk and that's temporary, but you're a bloody fool and that's permanent.[15]

Care was taken to fill the bottle up to the bung, to prevent the cider swillicking as the bottle was carried, and becoming flat. A little cider was poured on the ground before drinking, even in the present century; and the cider was drunk either directly from the costrel, from a leather mug or blackjack, or from a horn: "swipe your horn" was the encouragement given by a thirsty labourer to the man who dallied with the communal horn. When cider was drawn directly from the barrel, in the evening after work, it was also common for a single horn to be used, and passed from one man to another after being refilled; it would pass thus round the little circle who surrounded the tap, always in a clockwise direction, just as the port circulates in senior combination rooms of the better Cambridge colleges, and in the same direction as every stone cider mill in Herefordshire.

Notes

PART ONE

[1] Radcliffe Cooke, C. W., *A Book about Cider and Perry*, London, 1898, pp. 3, 4. The Saxon conquest of Britain obliterated most of the place names of the country, more so in the east (where the conquest was complete by A.D. 550) than in the west (which was not subjugated until about 800). The result is that few if any surviving British place names afford evidence of the culture of the apple or pear. However, the advancing Saxons named their settlements both after their own leaders and from features of the countryside, and we may suppose that Saxon names containing a word for "apple" or "pear" represent an old cultivated orchard or outstanding wild trees, from which no doubt a drink of some sort was made. The word "perry" on its own or in combination with other elements occurs in Huntingdonshire, Kent, Oxfordshire and Staffordshire: it is derived from the Old English *pirige*, "pear tree". The word for "pear", *peru*, is found in the names Parbold, Parham, Parley, Preshaw and Prested. Names founded on the existence of apple tree are more frequent: Apley in Lincolnshire is the Old English *aeppel-leah*, "apple wood", as is Apperly in Gloucestershire; Appleton in Berkshire is derived from a word that is also recorded as meaning simply "orchard". We cannot now tell whether "apple wood" meant "uncultivated apple trees" and was opposed to the cultivated "orchard", but it seems unlikely. Probably all of these were orchards of what after all was a Roman province. The Old English name for a single apple tree was *apuldor*, which survives directly as Appledore, in Dorset. See Ekwall, E., *The Concise Oxford Dictionary of English Place-Names*, Oxford, 1960, (4th ed.).

[2] Stopes, H., *Cider. The History, Method of Manufacture and Properties of this National Beverage*, London, 1888, p. 7.

[3] Harvey, W., *Lectures on the Whole of Anatomy*, ed. C. D. O'Malley *et al.*, University of California Press, 1961, p. 86.

[4] For example, Worlidge, J., *Vinetum Britannicum: or, a Treatise of Cider...*, London, 1676, preface.

[5] Sylvius, J., *In Hippocatis et Galeni Physiologiae partem Anatomicam Isagoge*, Venice, 1556, p. 10v.

[6] Singer, C., *et al.*, *A History of Technology*, Oxford, 1956, Vol. 1, p. 139.

[7] Stopes, *op. cit.*, p. 8.

[8] Derry, T. K., and Williams, T. I., *A Short History of Technology*, Oxford, 1960, p. 61.

[9] McConaghey, R. M. S., "Sir George Baker and the Devonshire colic", *Medical History*, II (1967), 345–60.

[10] Salzmann, L. F., *English Industries in the Middle Ages*, London, 1913, p. 197.

[11] *Ibid.*, p. 197.

[12] Worlidge, J., *Mr. Worlidge's two treatises* (No. 2, the second part of the *Vinetum Britannicum*), London, 1694, p. 106.

[13] Turner, T. Hudson, *Some account of Domestic Architecture in Britain from the Conquest to the end of the Thirteenth Century*, Oxford, 1851, Vol. 1, p. 139.

[14] Parkinson, J., *Paradisi in sole Paradisus Terestris*, London, 1629, p. 589.

[15] *Oxford English Dictionary.*

[16] Gaut, R. C., *A History of Worcestershire Agriculture and Rural Evolution*, Worcester, 1939, p. 75.

[17] Markham, G., *A Way to get Wealth: containing sixe Principall Vocations or callings in which every Husband or Housewife may carefully imploy themselves*, London, 1648 (7th ed.).

[18] Newburgh in Evelyn, J., *Pomona*, London, 1706.

[19] *Ibid.*, p. 86.

[20] Mr Cook, *ibid.*, p. 121.

[21] *Ibid.*, p. 127.

[22] See, for example, Hale, T., *A Compleat Body of Husbandry*, London, 1756, p. 615, and Stafford, H., *A Treatise on Cyder-Making*, London, 1759, p. 50, and Mr Cook in Evelyn's *Pomona*, p. 122.

[23] Evelyn, *op. cit.*, p. 59.

[24] See Hale, *op. cit.*, p. 615, and Stafford, *op. cit.*, p. 50.

[25] See, for example, Ellis, W., *The Compleat Cyderman*, London, 1754. The French made a similar distinction between cyder, *le gros cidre* or *le cidre paré* (if still slightly sweet), and *le petit cidre*, small cider made by regrinding the murc (*le marc*) together with water. *Le petit cidre* was the normal drink of the French peasant. Details may be found in Diderot's *Encyclopédie*, Paris, 1753, Vol. 3, "Cidre".

[26] Robinson, B., *A Treatise of the Animal Oeconomy*, Dublin, 1733, p. 238.

[27] This analysis appears in the ninth edition of the *Encyclopaedia Britannica* (1876): weights are in avoirdupois grains. Water 8292.41; alcohol 367.69; sugar 31.67; gums 45.05; albumen 1.95; malic acid 44.86; residue 18.38.

[28] *The English Cyclopedia*, London, 1859. Vol. 2: article "Cider".

[29] Fox, Sir Cyril and Raglan, Lord, *Monmouthshire Houses*, Cardiff, 1953, part 2, p. 84.

[30] Fox and Raglan, *op. cit.*, give as an example Parc-Grace-Dieu in Monmouthshire. Lower Gockett in the same county is a medieval farmhouse to which a cyder house was added in the eighteenth century.

[31] Barley, M. W., *The English Farmhouse and Cottage*, London, 1961, p. 156.

[32] Norden, J., *The Surveiors Dialogue*, London, 1610, p. 168.

[33] Gibson, E., ed., *Camden's Britannia newly translated into English*, London, 1695, pp. 574, 579.

[34] Worlidge, *Vinetum Britannicum* . . . .

[35] Cyder fruit was normally sold by the sack, each of which contained four corn bushels, about the produce of a mature tree. One-and-six or two shillings was a common price at the end of the seventeenth century for a sack of apples. In the earlier eighteenth century the price ranged from two shillings to six shillings; it was, for example, two-and-eightpence in 1748. See Evelyn, *op. cit.*, pp. 58, 77, and Worlidge, *Vinetum Britannicum*. See also Haines, R., *Aphorisms on the new way of improving Cyder*, London, 1684, p. 7. These authors also discuss the price of finished cyder, suggesting profits of up to £25 per acre; but they are all advocates of cyder making and have probably chosen unrepresentatively high prices.

[36] Ellis, *op. cit.*, p. 11.

[37] To rent "a little Orchard, with a Hutt of a house to it" cost fifty shillings a year, and might be expected to produce ten hogsheads: Ellis, *op. cit.*, p. 56. In calculating the investment and profit of the seventeenth- and eighteenth-century cyderist no account has been taken here of the cost of installing a mill, which once set up lasted for centuries. Nevertheless the installer of the mill probably expected to see some return on his outlay, reckoned at £20–30 at the end of the seventeenth century, taking into account the room in which it was housed. See Worlidge, *Mr Worlidge's two treatises*, p. 124.

[38] *The Code of Agriculture, including Observations on Gardens, Orchards, Woods and Plantations*, London, 1817, p. 428.

[39] Haines, *op. cit.*, Worlidge, *Vinetum Britannicum* . . ., and McConaghey, *op. cit.*

[40] Ellis in the *Compleat Cyderman* records the Herefordshire hogshead as 64, 70, 80 or 110 gallons. The volume of the hogshead varied from county to county and in time, at least in Hereford, tended to settle at the larger measure. In the century before Ellis wrote, Haines gives us 60 gallons as the volume of a hogshead (in 1684), and contemporary sources record 64. Ellis himself gives evidence that the Bedfordshire hogshead was 63 gallons. Twenty years after the publication of Ellis's

book, that great monument to learning, the *Encyclopédie* of Diderot, gave with Gallic precision the volume of a French hogshead as 168 "tankards" or 488 litres. This is close to the 110 gallons to which the hogshead tended in the eighteenth century. By the end of the century the Herefordshire cider dealers determined the price of cider according to a hogshead of 110 gallons, and in the nineteenth-century it seems clear that the volume had settled at between 100 and 110 gallons; noted for example by Radcliffe Cooke.

[41] See Sinclair, *op. cit.*, p. 432, and below, where the techniques of making cyder are discussed.

[42] Worlidge, *Mr Worlidge's two treatises*, preface.

[43] Clark-Kennedy, E., *Stephen Hales, DD, FRS. An eighteenth-century biography*, Cambridge, 1929, p. 182.

[44] Quoted by Gaut, *op. cit.*, p. 304.

[45] Knight, T. A., *A Treatise on the Culture of the Apple and Pear and on the Manufacture of Cider and Perry*, Ludlow, 1809, p. 104.

[46] Women were paid just half of this amount. Gaut, *op. cit.*, p. 181.

[47] *Ibid.* p. 241.

[48] Turner's account of Gloucestershire in 1794, in Marshall, W., *The Review and Abstracts of the County Reports to the Board of Agriculture*, 5 vols; vol 2, 1818.

[49] The report on North Somerset in Marshall, *op. cit.*

[50] Quoted by M. B. Quinion, *A Drink for its Time. Farm Cider Making in the Western Counties*, Hereford, 1979. Mr Quinion is Curator of the Museum of Cider, Hereford.

[51] Gaut, *op. cit.*, p. 358.

[52] *Ibid.*, p. 399.

[53] *Ibid.*, p. 194.

[54] Ellis, *op. cit.*, p. 56.

[55] Some anonymous, some signed. For example, Heath, B. (The Recorder of Exeter), *The Case of the County of Devon, with respect to the Consequences of the new Excise Duty on Cyder and Perry*, 1763. Thomas Alcock, vicar of Runcorn, who was to become involved in the debate about Devon cider as a cause of lead poisoning (see below) produced in 1763 *Observations on that Part of a late Act of Parliament, which lays an Additional Duty to Cider and Perry*. Anonymous publications of the same year include *An Address to Honest English Hearts . . .*, *Some Plain Reasons for the Repeal of the Cider Act . . .*, and others to be found in Watt, R., *Bibliotheca Britannica*, Edinburgh, 1824. (Vol. 3, under "Cyder".)

[56] Ellis, *op. cit.*, p. 91.

[57] The Herefordshire mill is normally a solid disc of stone, constructed thus, with the trough running round its edge. Apples for milling are normally piled up on the centre of the base of the mill, around the central post, and are "rowed down" into the trough after the horse has

passed. Larger mills elsewhere have a cavity around the central post for the storage of apples.

[58] Dr A. Keller, Dept. History of Science, University of Leicester (private communication).

[59] Ellis, *op. cit.*, p. 95.

[60] Zonca, V., *Novo Theatro di Machine et Edificii*, Padua, 1656.

[61] Diderot, *op. cit.*

[62] Blumner, H., *Technologie und Terminologie der Gewerbe und Kunste bei Griechern und Romern*, Leipzig, 1912, p. 351.

[63] A water-driven scratter is to be found at Rowlstone Mill, near Pontrilas. It is in working order at the time of writing and cider was made with it in 1976.

[64] Worlidge describes the ingenio in his books of 1676 and 1694.

[65] See Evelyn in the Introduction to his *Pomona*; an eighteenth-century example is the Rev. G. Turner in Hale, *op. cit.*

[66] See the account by Webster, C., *The Great Instauration. Science, Medicine and Reform, 1626–1660*, London, 1975.

[67] Quoted from Webster, *op. cit.*

[68] It was delivered to the Royal Society in 1662 and the first edition appeared in 1664. Modifications to the text were made by Evelyn at least up to the 3rd edition of 1678, largely as a result of incorporating material contributed by readers of the Royal Society's *Philosophical Transactions*, where Evelyn advertised for information in 1666. The edition of 1706 has been used here.

[69] A "Mr Hake", conceivably Theodore Haak.

[70] MacDonell, A., ed., *The Closet of Sir Kenelm Digby Knight Opened*, London, 1910, p. 100, contains a curious recipe for concentrating, by boiling, a sliced-apple *dépense*.

[71] The mixture was punningly (by a "designed equivocation") called pearmaine cider. *Philosophical Transactions of the Royal Society* Vol. 43 (1744–5), p. 516: "Extract of a letter from the Reverend Henry MILES DD and FRS to the President, relating to some Improvements which may be made in Cyder and Perry" (with the purpose of encouraging planting on waste ground).

[72] Haines, *op. cit.*

[73] See, for example, Parkinson, *op. cit.*, and Ham, J., *The Manufacture of Cider and Perry reduced to Rules*, Sherborne, 1828, pp. 49, 50.

[74] Worlidge, *Mr Worlidge's two treatises*, p. 131, suggested that Haines's method was used in conjunction with the addition of molasses or treacle, to improve poor cider, not to produce a substitute for brandy. Distillation is also discussed by Beale. See Evelyn, *op. cit.*, pp. 94 and 114.

[75] Boorde, A., *A Dyetary of Helth* (1542), reprinted by the Early English Text Society, London, 1870, p. 256.

[76] Lawson, W., *A new Orchard, and Garden*, London, 1648, p. 67.

[77] Parkinson, *op. cit.*, p. 589 *et seq.*

[78] Evelyn, *op. cit.*, p. 59.

[79] Herefordshire was known for the longevity of its inhabitants at least as early as the middle of the seventeenth century. Beale attributes it to the apple trees purifying the air. Beale, J., *Herefordshire Orchards, a Pattern for all England* (1656), London, 1724, p. 5.

[80] Bull, H. G. and Hogg, R., eds., *The Herefordshire Pomona*, 2 vols., 1876–85.

[81] Willis, T., *Pharmaceutice Rationalis*, The Hague, 1675, p. 422.

[82] This information is taken from the manuscript Minute Books of the Aberdeen Infirmary, which begin in 1742.

[83] An excellent survey of the literature is given by Lind. See Stewart, C. P., and Guthrie, D., eds., *Lind's Treatise on Scurvy*, Edinburgh, 1953.

[84] Roddis, L. H., *James Lind*, London, 1951, p. 44.

[85] Quoted by Stopes, *op. cit.*, p. 13.

[86] Bacon, F., *Sylva Sylvarum* (together with *New Atlantis*), 7th ed., London, 1658, pp. 2, 5, 12.

[87] Parkinson, *op. cit.*, p. 589.

[88] H[enry] P[latt] *Certain Philosophical Preparations of Food and Beverage for Sea-men, in their long Voyages....* The copy in the Wellcome Library has "1607. Sᵣ Henry Platt" in a contemporary hand. Other sources suggest the Christian name Hugh.

[89] Evelyn, *op. cit.*, p. 128.

[90] Stewart, and Guthrie, eds., *op. cit.*, p. 147.

[91] Eddy, W., and Dalldorf, G., *The Avitaminoses*, London, 1941.

[92] See Stewart, Mieklejohn and Passmore in Stewart and Guthrie, eds., *op. cit.*, p. 434.

[93] McCance, R. A., and Widdowson, E. M., *The Composition of Foods*, London, H.M.S.O., 1960, quoted by R. E. Hughes, "James Lind and the cure of scurvy: an experimental approach". *Medical History, 19* (1975), 342–51.

[94] Hughes, *op. cit.*

[95] *Ibid.*

[96] I am deeply indebted for these figures to Dr Paul Luzio of the Department of Clinical Biochemistry in the University of Cambridge.

[97] Stewart and Guthrie, eds., *op. cit.*

[98] Quoted by McConaghey, *op. cit.*

[99] In Stafford, *op. cit.*, p. 70, it is recommended that its use be restricted to meals; unrestricted use leads even to death.

[100] Some indication of the size of the industry is given by the fact that in good years at the middle of the century at Plumtree, near Exeter, the number of hogsheads made was three times the total population. See Stafford, *op. cit.*, p. IV.

[101] Ellis, *op. cit.*
[102] Stafford, *op. cit.*, pp. 50, 61.
[103] See also Ham, *op. cit.*, p. 28.
[104] See the account of the cyder given by Captain Sylas Taylor in Evelyn, *op. cit.*

PART TWO

[1] See Uttley, J., *The Story of the Channel Islands*, London, 1966, pp. 99, 132, 141. The modern firm of Aspall originated with the shipping of a large granite cyder mill from the Channel Islands to Suffolk in about 1720.

[2] *Georgics III*, 273.

[3] Philips and a number of contributors to Evelyn's *Pomona*, London, 1706: Sylas Taylor, Beale and Colwall.

[4] Sylas Taylor in Evelyn, *op. cit.* Philips's poem follows *Pomona* closely on this subject, and his words recall very strongly Beale's treatise.

[5] Also in the Woolhope Dome is the village of Much Marcle, the home of the modern firm of Weston's, and the site of the "Wonder" landslip of 1571 (Gibson, E., ed., *Camden's Britannia newly translated into English*, London, 1695, pp. 574, 579) when the slippery shale carried whole orchards intact over neighbouring grazing, "affording", as Philips observed, "matter strange/For law debates...." The hillier parts of the Woolhope Dome, particularly around the village of Checkley, are difficult to farm on a large scale, and the small and steep fields have resisted the changes that turned the flatter fields of more easterly counties into prairies. Here the old mills and presses of the heyday of cider making are more numerous, many forgotten in overgrown corners, but some still used. This is one of the last places in Herefordshire, and therefore in the world, where visitors are offered a horn of cider.

[6] There is a country saying:
"He that planteth perry pears
Truly planteth for his heirs."

[7] Stopes, H., *Cider. The History, Method of Manufacture and Properties of this National Beverage*, London, 1888, p. 19.

[8] Turner, T. Hudson, *Some account of Domestic Architecture in Britain from the Conquest to the end of the Thirteenth Century*, Oxford, 1851, Vol. I, p. 136.

[9] See MacDonell A., ed., *The Closet of Sir Kenelm Digby Knight Opened*,

London, 1910, p. 101.

[10] Perhaps the story proves only the low quality of his own wine, for he was unable to drink his sack in quantities greater than sips or to drink his French wine without sugar.

[11] Evelyn, *op. cit.*, p. 86.

[12] *Ibid.*, p. 115.

[13] Worlidge, J., *Vinetum Britannicum: or, a Treatise of Cider...*, London, 1676, p. 76.

[14] Evelyn, *op. cit.*, p. 108.

[15] Worlidge, *op. cit.*, p. 76.

[16] For example, Dr Smith in Evelyn, *op. cit.*, p. 114.

[17] *Ibid.*, p. 87.

[18] Worlidge, *op. cit.*, p. 78.

[19] Worlidge, *The Most Easie Method for Making the Best Cyder*, London, 1687, p. 4.

[20] For example, by Worlidge, *Vinetum Britannicum...*, p. 81. He was, of course, promoting his ingenio.

[21] See, for example, the discussions on the *Philosophical Transactions* of the Royal Society, Vols. 2 (1667), 502; 6 (1671), 2128; 43 (1744–5), 516.

[22] The Roman Ariconium was believed in Philips's time to be the modern Hereford.

[23] Bacon, F., *Of the Advancement and Proficiencie of Learning*, London, 1674, p. 148. The first edition was published in 1605.

[24] Worlidge, *Vinetum Britannicum...*, p. 89.

[25] Evelyn, *op. cit.*, p. 99.

[26] By Newburgh, *ibid.*, p. 111.

[27] See, for example, Stafford, H., *A Treatise on Cyder-Making*, London, 1759, p. 11, and Knight, T. A., *A Treatise on the Culture of the Apple and Pear and on the Manufacture of Cider and Perry*, Ludlow, 1809, p. 104.

[28] Worlidge, *Vinetum Britannicum...*, p. 88.

[29] Worlidge, *Mr Worlidge's two treatises*, 1694, p. 147.

[30] Carr, J. G., *Modern Methods of Cider Making*, published by the National Association of Cider Makers, n.d. (after 1966), p. 13.

[31] Hale, T., *A Compleat Body of Husbandry*, London, 1756, p. 615.

[32] Markham, G., *A Way to get Wealth: containing sixe Principall Vocations or callings in which every Husband or Housewife may carefully imploy themselves*, London, 1648 (7th ed.), p. 248.

[33] See, for example, Sir Paul Neile in Evelyn, *op. cit.*, p. 96. and John Newburgh, *ibid.*, p. 109.

[34] Worlidge, *Vinetum Britannicum...*, pp. 92–4, and *The Most Easie Method...*, p. 7.

[35] See, for example, Sir Paul Neile in Evelyn, *op. cit.*, p. 106.

[36] See the improbable story of Newburgh, *ibid.*, p. 109, which, however, reveals his belief in the activity of the spirit.

[37] Sir Paul Neile, *ibid.*, p. 100.
[38] See Dr Smith, *ibid.*, p. 114, and John Newburgh, *ibid.*, p. 113.
[39] See Beale, *ibid.*, p. 88.
[40] Worlidge, *Vinetum Britannicum* . . . , p. 117.
[41] Stafford, *op. cit.*, p. 56.
[42] See Knight, *op. cit.*, p. 101 and Ham, J., *The Manufacture of Cider and Perry reduced to Rules*, Sherborne, 1828, p. 11.
[43] Ellis, W., *The Compleat Cyderman*, London, 1754, p. 75.
[44] Evelyn, *op. cit.*, p. 115.
[45] *Ibid.* p. 94.
[46] Dr Smith, *ibid.*, p. 114.
[47] Worlidge, *Vinetum Britannicum* . . , p. 105.
[48] See Captain Sylas Taylor, Evelyn, *op. cit.*, p. 117.
[49] *Ibid.*, p. 109.
[50] The production of a sparkling wine and its improvement in bottle were no doubt discovered by accident as a natural result of bottling cyder to extend its life. Sir Paul Neile has a story of a Herefordshire gentleman who, "dispatching a *Barque* for London" with cyder, found he had more cyder than wooden vessels to fill and was obliged to send a quantity in corked bottles. The barque was delayed some two months upon its journey when the superiority of the bottled cyder was very evident. (Evelyn, *op. cit.*, p. 104.)
[51] Sir Paul Neile, in Evelyn, *op. cit.*, p. 101.
[52] Beale, *ibid.*, p. 88 and anon., *ibid.*, p. 122.
[53] Sir Paul Neile, *ibid.*, p. 101.
[54] See Beale, Sir Paul Neile and Cook in Evelyn, *op. cit.*, pp. 88, 101, 122; also Worlidge, *Vinetum Britannicum* . . . , p. 106.
[55] Drummond, J. C., *The Englishman's Food*, London, 1959, p. 113.
[56] *Ibid.*, p. 213.
[57] Worlidge, *Vinetum Britannicum* . . . , p. 103.
[58] *Ibid.*, p. 106.
[59] Evelyn, *op. cit.*, p. 94.
[60] Brande, W., and Cox, G., *A Dictionary of Science, Literature and Art*, London, 1865.
[61] Worlidge, *Vinetum Britannicum* . . . , p. 115.
[62] Ellis, *op. cit.*, p. 56.
[63] Worlidge, *Vinetum Britannicum* . . . , p. 116, and Sir Paul Neile in Evelyn, *op. cit.*, p. 97.
[64] Stafford, *op. cit.*, p. 58.
[65] Caused by lactic acid bacteria building up polysaccharides.
[66] Stafford, *op. cit.*, p. 61.

PART THREE
[1] Worlidge, J., *Vinetum Britannicum: or, a Treatise of Cider* . . . ,

London, 1676, p. 120.

[2] See, for example, Culpeper's mid-seventeenth century *Herbal*. The edition used here is the *Complete Herbal*, London, 1815. See pp. 155, 195.

[3] Stafford, H., *A Treatise on Cyder-Making*, London, 1759, p. 61.

[4] Culpeper, *op. cit.*, p. 50.

[5] *Philosophical Transactions*, Vol. 2, no. 27 (Sept. 1667), p. 501.

[6] McDouall, Robin, *Cooking with Wine*, Penguin, 1968.

[7] Partridge, E., *A Dictionary of Historical Slang*, London, 1972, and *Lexicon Balatronicum*, London, 1811.

[8] MacDonell, A., ed., *The Closet of Sir Kenelm Digby Knight Opened*, London, 1910.

[9] *Ibid.*, p. 97, and Worlidge, *op. cit.*, p. 128.

[10] See Worlidge, *op. cit.*, p. 128.

[11] Leather, E. M., *The Folk-Lore of Herefordshire*, 1973 (facsimile reprint of the edition of Hereford, 1912), p. 88.

[12] *Ibid.*, p. 92.

[13] Haggard, A., *Dialect and Local Usages of Herefordshire*, London, 1972, p. 48. On the dialect, see also Leeds, W., *Herefordshire Speech*, n.p., 1972.

[14] A nineteenth-century term used elsewhere for sour beer. See Partridge, *op. cit.*

[15] Haggard, *op. cit.*, p. 49.

Index